BUSHIDO CAPITALISM

THE CODE TO REDEFINE BUSINESS FOR A
SUSTAINABLE FUTURE

KENGO SAKURADA

D0708732

Published by
LID Publishing Limited
The Record Hall, Studio 304,
16-16a Baldwins Gardens,
London EC1N 7RJ, UK

info@lidpublishing.com
www.lidpublishing.com

A member of:

BPR ✹
businesspublishersroundtable.com

All rights reserved. Without limiting the rights under copyright reserved,
no part of this publication may be reproduced, stored or introduced into a
retrieval system, or transmitted, in any form or by any means (electronic,
mechanical, photocopying, recording or otherwise) without the prior written
permission of both the copyright owners and the publisher of this book.

© Kengo Sakurada, 2021
© LID Publishing Limited, 2021

Printed by CPI Group (UK) Ltd, Croydon CR0 4YY

ISBN: 978-1-911671-58-9
ISBN: 978-1-911671-59-6 (ebook)

Cover and page design: Caroline Li

BUSHIDO CAPITALISM

THE CODE TO REDEFINE BUSINESS FOR A
SUSTAINABLE FUTURE

KENGO SAKURADA

MADRID | MEXICO CITY | LONDON
NEW YORK | BUENOS AIRES
BOGOTA | SHANGHAI | NEW DELHI

To future generations:
You inspire us to become better
versions of ourselves.

CONTENTS

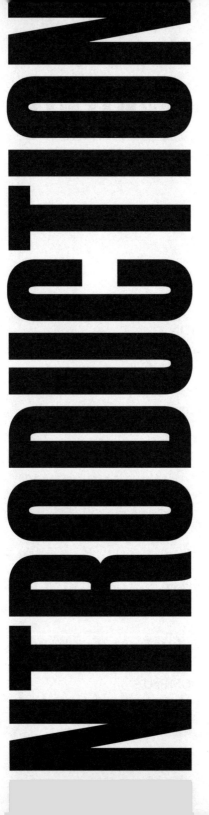

INTRODUCTION

OPPORTUNITY IN CRISIS

I was an obstinate boy. It is not something I'm particularly proud of, but when I was growing up, I was thoroughly anti-authoritarian and uncooperative. I was moody and perhaps a little belligerent. I staked out my own path, questioned rules and regulations and generally refused to abide by them.

I also had a seemingly endless supply of energy, but I didn't consider channeling it into productive or noble pursuits. Instead, outside of school hours, my friends and I would play juvenile pranks on each other. We would roast frogs in homemade charcoal ovens or play precariously close to the train line despite our parents' stern warnings. We were naive about the dangers or just thrilled by the risk.

My mother recalls a friend of hers once saying she had banned her own son from playing with me. "When my son spends the day with Kengo," she told my poor mother, "he's so exhausted by the evening, he can't even stay awake for dinner."

Although I mellowed a little with age, the rebel in me persevered. I started studying at Waseda University in Shinjuku, Tokyo, in 1974, and spent most of my first two years fooling around with my girlfriend and avoiding classes. That girlfriend is now my wife of more than 40 years, so while there is no way I can claim I wasted my time, academically I had little to show for it.

I was determined to only study what I wanted. When, in my third year, one of my classes covered the work of John Maynard Keynes, it was extremely fortuitous that my academic requirements and my selective interests converged. Detecting my newfound enthusiasm, my teacher recommended I read the original version of *The General Theory of Employment, Interest, and Money*, Keynes' final work and arguably one of his most influential.[1]

My English was not proficient at the time, and the complexity of the subject matter meant I had my work cut out for me. Aided by a Japanese translation of the book, I tackled the task head-on and soon started reading in earnest. I was hooked.

First, I was deeply impressed by how Keynes boldly challenged the entrenched economic theories that had, up until that point, been widely accepted as the absolute and only truth. His thinking paved the way for an entirely new approach to the study of economics by introducing novel theories on the interplay of labour markets, inflation and macroeconomics. I was in awe of his ability to scrutinize and criticize the great thinkers who had come before him. I was hungry to learn much more.

One of Keynes' stipulations that particularly captivated me during that early reading of *The General Theory of Employment, Interest, and Money* was the following: *"In the field of economic and political philosophy, there are not many who are influenced by new theories after they are 25 or 30 years of age."*

I was 21 at the time and, while the assertion made sense, it scared me. Did I only have a handful of years left to determine and shape who I would be for the rest of my life?

Decades later, I still reflect on this. Considering how far I have come since I was a young, defiant student, how many experiences I've lived and how much knowledge I've acquired, you might think Keynes was mistaken. But he wasn't entirely.

There is some truth to his claim. I am still profoundly influenced by the theories I learned and absorbed as a young man. High school and university Kengo is still present, but countless new layers have been added since. Importantly, I have come to learn that it's never too late to add an extra layer, to be influenced by a new theory, to be challenged in a new way and to look at things in a wholly different light.

To really succeed in this complex world, we must be able to bend without breaking. We must flex every day and in everything that we do. As Keynes argued, we may never be able to change who we are at our core, but no one is ever too old to develop and to adapt to the world around them. It's never been more important to appreciate this truth.

As I've evolved over the years, many things have shaped and guided me. I've had mentors and friends, colleagues and competitors, who have all challenged me to become a better version of Kengo, but there's one book that I have considered to be an overarching road map – a moral compass, if you like – that I've consulted ahead of every big decision I've ever had to make.

In April 1904, Theodore Roosevelt wrote a letter to Kentaro Kaneko. In it, the 26th president of the United States thanked the Japanese statesman and diplomat profusely for a book that he had recently received as a gift. "It seems to me, my dear Baron, that Japan has much to teach the Occident," he wrote.

The book that Roosevelt was referring to – and that I've come to treasure so much - was a slim volume that had been published a few years earlier, entitled *Bushido: The Soul of Japan*.[2]

Penned by the educator, diplomat and agricultural economist Inazo Nitobe, the book interprets the Japanese Samurai code of behaviour and explains how chivalrous men should act in their personal and professional lives. Bushido, he explains in the first section of the book, "is the code of moral principles which the Knights were required or instructed to observe."

As I reflect upon the ways in which capitalism must change in order to be a force for the common good, I can't help but think about Nitobe's principles of Bushido and the extent to which – if molded and adapted – they provide a framework and moral compass for all of us today.

We have thankfully evolved since the 1900s, and some of Nitobe's rhetoric and vernacular is simply no longer appropriate and relevant, but I wholeheartedly subscribe to the spirit of the book.

Bushido has shaped my values and belief systems during every phase of my career, and I believe that it can serve as an invaluable resource far beyond the borders of Japan as we enter this new era of capitalism.

TO SUCCEED IN THIS COMPLEX WORLD, WE MUST BE ABLE TO BEND WITHOUT BREAKING.

AN INFLECTION POINT

The world we live in has been pushed to its absolute limits. After several decades of rapid innovation and acceleration, supply chains and travel came to a jarring halt in 2020, as the global pandemic ricocheted across every continent.

Consumers who had become accustomed to an on-demand way of living – where trans-Pacific trips could be made on a whim and almost anything purchased at the click of a button – were forced into a socially distanced reality.

An existence defined by never-ending optionality – what to buy, where to go, who to see and how to live – was streamlined dramatically overnight. Remote working and face masks in public necessarily became the norm. Heads of state were challenged in entirely unexpected ways. Healthcare systems in many cases became the preeminent concern for the young and healthy, in a way they had previously only been for the old and frail.

The shockwaves of the pandemic reverberated through practically every organization, in every country, both in the public and private sector. Employers were challenged to assume a far more consequential duty of care for their staff and workers. The term *responsible business* – once an aspirational catch-all rolled out for marketing purposes – rapidly took on a whole new set of meanings.

But while the pandemic seemed to transform the way we live, work, consume and socialize, it was not in itself a cause of great change; rather, it was a catalyst.

In the broadest sense, this book examines how we got to this point in history, how we can use this forced pause to reassess and recalibrate, and how business leaders across all industries should leverage power and influence to rebuild a new version of capitalism that is responsive, agile, ethical, sustainable and unconditionally resilient.

Though it is easy to refer to the current global dynamic as unprecedented, a glance through the history books suggests otherwise. Global systems – financial markets, political regimes and social forces – have always moved in cycles. Almost like clockwork, systems have repeatedly flourished, failed and then thrived again.

In their 1991 book, *Generations: The History of America's Future, 1584 to 2069*,[3] William Strauss and Neil Howe theorize that each generation belongs to one of four types, and that each type recurs sequentially in a fixed pattern. Others have analysed or attempted to explain the commonly perceived sense of historical deja vu by drawing on behavioural science.

The availability heuristic, coined by psychologists Amos Tversky and Daniel Kahneman,[4] for example, refers to the human brain computing and processing certain things by drawing on past experiences, beliefs, judgments or decisions. It explains why humans tend to resort to behavioural patterns that are familiar: why we so commonly make the same mistake over and over again.

More recently, short-termism has proved a popular explanation. Academics, think tanks, labour unions and even heads of state have blamed overly myopic business leaders for the shortcomings of free market economies, giving rise to terms like *quarterly capitalism*, popularized by Hillary Clinton.[5]

However intently we study the past, and however forensically we analyse our historical missteps, we won't break the patterns of boom-and-bust and rise-and-fall that have endured for centuries. But as we emerge from the latest global crisis, striking for both its magnitude and its truly global reach, there are unique lessons we can learn.

Never has the world seen such an extraordinary degree of convergence during a crisis: the economy, transport networks, healthcare systems and social orders were all blindsided simultaneously and forced to adapt entirely.

Across three sections – Great Acceleration, Forced Pause and Recalibrating Capitalism – this book endeavours to make sense of how we got here, what it means and where we can go next to stop ourselves from repeating our mistakes.

First, it examines how the Great Acceleration materialized, what fueled it, and in what ways it might have gone too far. It scrutinizes certain parameters and norms, and questions whether individuals, businesses and communities are measuring success in the most conducive way. Has our obsession with speed and size gotten out of hand? Plenty of examples from recent years suggest it has. This book seeks to help readers understand why that is, and what – if anything – we can do about it.

Second, we consider the Forced Pause. This section reflects on how crises – like pandemics, economic depressions and wars – can be used as opportunities to reflect and reset. Specifically, it examines the role business leaders can play when systems are disrupted unexpectedly and sometimes irreversibly.

The third part explores how we can recalibrate capitalism, how we need to make the most of this period of reflection and how we can rebuild and rebalance the system that we have been accustomed to for decades, in a way that is more responsible and more ethical.

Finally, the last section of the book is devoted to the notion of post-crisis recalibration and ways in which you, your organization and your community can contribute to creating a better stakeholder ecosystem. This section examines how sustainability can be achieved – both ecologically and economically – in a world in which populations are living far longer than they used to. It underscores the importance of accountability and transparency, of pragmatism and realism. It spells out ways in which innovation can be paced responsibly and implemented intelligently to achieve goals that have been on many business agendas for years: creating equality of opportunity within the workforce and an environment in which workers from four or even five different generations can support, promote and challenge each other in a dynamic way.

Throughout each chapter, I will refer to the values of Bushido, and I will draw on these principles – and what I consider to be

Japan's practical wisdoms – to suggest ways in which governments and corporations can work together to ensure that societal systems meet the needs of our rapidly evolving world.

Text boxes in each chapter will guide you through each virtue in the code of Bushido and provide examples of how you can apply this code to become the most responsible employee, manager or leader you can be.

The book is intended for businesspeople across all geographies and industries, and although it will not provide a panacea, or unequivocal answers, it will help you understand how we got to this point and the responsibilities we hold to devise a solution.

Business leaders are architects. It is their responsibility to design a sustainable future and to lead by example and in the interest of the common good. One way to do that is by developing and adhering to a framework that promotes environmental, social and corporate governance (ESG) factors. The values of Bushido can support businesses as they do so. As architects, this book is a tool that can help us perfect our valuable trade.

HAS OUR OBSESSION WITH SPEED AND SIZE GOT OUT OF HAND?

INTRODUCTION: SUMMARY

The world is facing an inflection point. In 2020, we witnessed an extraordinary degree of convergence: the economy, transport networks, healthcare systems and social orders were all struck simultaneously by the pandemic and were forced to adapt entirely.

This has reminded us of the importance of agility and being able to attempt and bend without breaking.

As we prepare ourselves for the post-pandemic world, Inazo Nitobe's book, *Bushido: The Soul of Japan*, can be a valuable guide. It was originally written as the code of moral principles that the Samurai were required to observe but, considered through the lens of our modern world, it can help us to be more responsible, ethical and better leaders.

1

GREAT
ACCELERATION

I was born in Suginami, a part of Tokyo, in February 1956. I could write a whole library on the innovations that have transformed our world since then but, for now, I will consider the most dramatic and consequential developments from the last two decades.

In the relatively short period since the dawn of the new millennium, we have radically changed the way we interact with each other. Barriers to global travel have, in many places, vanished entirely. Budget airlines have thrived, and transport networks have become more efficient. The internet has evolved from being a domain reserved for the academic, or technologically brilliant, to being a home for almost two-thirds of the global population,[6] regardless of socioeconomic status.

Smartphones have transformed from communication gadgets to being our around-the-clock companions. Mobile internet users account for around 90% of total internet users[7] today, and one study in 2020 showed that attachment anxiety to mobile phones is a real and increasingly prevalent phenomena, particularly among young people.[8]

All of these observations suggest we have been witnessing a 'Great Acceleration' over the last century: while the world keeps spinning on its axis at the same pace as it has done for millennia, everything happening on the surface of our small planet has been speeding up exponentially, with the most dramatic changes occurring in the last 20 years.

One of the biggest consequences is that we have become accustomed to an on-demand way of living. Platform economies have made it easy for many of us to summon almost any product or service at the simple touch of a button. Corporations are jostling to secure an edge by trying to anticipate our next whim or wish before we even know what it is going to be. Over just a few years, companies like Amazon and Uber have changed from obscure niche service providers to enjoying absolute ubiquity in many countries.

Growth has been relentless. Businesses now draw in quarterly revenues that surpass the gross domestic product of many states. Individual wealth has soared because of corporate might, availability of cash and market dynamics.

From March 2009 to March 2020, global stock indices were on a constant upward trajectory, a bull market – in financial parlance – that was completely unprecedented in terms of duration.[9] From trough to peak, that run awarded investors a return of more than 400%, mostly on account of record-low interest rates fueling a furious global hunt for yield.

It is human nature to associate speed and growth with victory. Exuberance and abundance are often associated with success. Consider the phrase "the bigger, the better." We are awed by the rapid growth of company profits without considering how they might have come about and at what cost. Recent research found that Americans even tend to presume that being bigger – or, in this case, taller – confers advantages in the workplace.[10]

But as we become accustomed to a hyperconnected, supercharged world where superlatives reign, it is also apparent that the effects of the Great Acceleration are not all good. Most should make us deeply uncomfortable.

INEQUALITY

Predictably, on account of rapid globalization and huge technological leaps, wealth inequality has increased alarmingly over recent years. The richest 1% in the world now have more than double the wealth of 6.9 billion people[11] and, as of 2020, the world's richest 22 men had more money than all the women in Africa combined.

The acclaimed late labour economist Alan Krueger made a speech in 2012 coining the term *The Great Gatsby Curve* to underscore the link between concentration of wealth in one generation, and the inability of those in subsequent generations to move up the socioeconomic ladder.[12] He argued that inequality now breeds inequality later. Though Krueger's remarks pertained to the US labour market, his theory is globally relevant.

A deep wealth gap still exists and, in many countries, racial divides have been fomented by developments that have concentrated money and power in the hands of the few.

In the US, where income inequality is the highest of all the G7 nations, households in the top fifth of earners were bringing in

52% of all US income, as of early 2020. This was more than the lower four-fifths combined.[13]

THE FIRST VIRTUE OF BUSHIDO: RECTITUDE OR JUSTICE

In many ways, this is the strongest virtue of Bushido, underpinning all others and providing a moral and ethical bedrock. It describes an individual's ability and power to make decisions and take actions based on reason and without hesitation and that are in the interest of the many. This virtue is about the common good of society, and one particularly salient example of this virtue lies in the Japanese business principle of *Sampo-Yoshi*.

Sampo-Yoshi encompasses the notion of success through responsibility. It means achieving three-way satisfaction: it is advantageous for the seller, but also for the buyer and for the broader society. Sampo-Yoshi means that a business owes its customers and communities success and that it therefore has to prioritize citizenship in everything it does.

This virtue provides an anchor and structure for the rest of the code of conduct. Without rectitude or justice, every other virtue is powerless. It is uncompromisable for Samurais – just as it should be for today's business leaders and responsible citizens.

To me, this concept includes the creation of diversification in the workplace where no one is judged by – or reduced to – a defining characteristic or personality trait. It ensures that every employee, regardless of gender, belief, religion, race, socioeconomic background or appearance, is evaluated by the product of their work and their dedication to their organization's wider mission.

As I mentioned in the first part of this book, the Great Acceleration and the pandemic have both plied open the equality gap across organizations, communities and countries. Wealth has, over recent decades, become even more concentrated in the hands of the rich, while the poor have languished. Elsewhere, the pandemic has disproportionately affected women, who have taken on far more domestic and caring duties than their male counterparts as schools and childcare facilities have shut.[14] Across many countries, including the US, hospitalizations, death and infection rates have been much higher among Black, Latino and Asian communities than among White communities.[15]

Widening equality gaps have significant implications for macroeconomic stability and disastrous social consequences. Research by the International Monetary Fund has shown that it can concentrate political and decision-making power in the hands of a few and "lead to a suboptimal use of human resources, cause investment-reducing political and economic instability, and raise crisis risk."[16]

We cannot let the pandemic-induced pause set us back and erase any progress that we've made.

As business leaders, it is a basic, fundamental duty to recognize that this first virtue of Bushido should be the centrepiece of our entire corporate value system.

Inequality extends far beyond economics. Access to education, healthcare and social services is still deeply uneven around the globe. For many of us who work in stable professions and live in metropolitan cities, being able to see a doctor or send our child to school seems a basic right and a privilege we are fortunate enough to take for granted. For billions around the world, the same is not true. As of 2019, almost 100 million people were pushed into extreme poverty annually because of out-of-pocket health expenses.[17]

It is easy, from this position of privilege, to avoid uncomfortable facts, but it's precisely our tendency to look the other way that makes the situation worse every year.

I have noted on many occasions that capitalism has lifted countless people out of poverty.[18] Yet it remains incumbent upon us not to allow those stories of heartening success to distract us from the urgent work – and the moral obligation – we face today.

THE
ENVIRONMENT

The environment has been another undisputed victim of the Great Acceleration. As supply chains and transport networks have expanded and become more complex, carbon emissions have soared and our natural resources are literally being burnt at an unprecedented rate. The earth's average surface temperature has risen by about 2 degrees Fahrenheit, or just over 1 degree Celsius, since the late 19th century, mostly driven by an increase in carbon dioxide and other man-made emissions into the atmosphere. Most of that warming occurred in the past four decades and many of the warmest periods on record have occurred since 2014. In 2016, eight months of the year – from January through September, with the exception of June – were the warmest on record for those respective months.[19]

In 2019, I experienced my own awakening when I met a young woman named Greta Thunberg at the World Economic Forum's annual meeting in Davos. I had barely heard of her and immediately tried to joke about something trivial. She did not laugh. Thunberg was in Davos for one very specific reason and she was angry at people like me – businesspeople who had failed to address a crisis now threatening the future of every generation to come.

Later in the day, Thunberg's speech on climate change seemed to silence the whole conference, and rightly so.[20] "Our house is on fire," the Swedish teenager said, and "don't steal our future."

It was haunting and deeply, necessarily uncomfortable. She taught me – and hopefully many of my peers – one of the most important lessons I will ever learn: we must listen to young people and truly hear them. We must trust them and give them the means and power to take matters into their own hands because they know what must be done.

Thunberg represents a promising new generation of brave activists who have the passion and resolve to make massive changes to benefit us all. Those who came before her can learn as much as those who follow in her footsteps. I will forever be grateful that I was able to meet her on that chilly day in the Swiss Alps, even though she did not laugh at my jokes.

Pressured by Thunberg and other campaigners, leaders across every industry have vowed to clean up their act, set an example and consider the interests of future generations. Unfortunately, few have taken meaningful steps. Shareholder primacy is still the status quo across many large corporations. Managers may have a green agenda but – perhaps distracted by the whirlwind of the Great Acceleration, by the illusory charm of speed, size and success – few have made the environment the cornerstone of their corporate strategy.

Worse still, some have resorted to tokenism or greenwashing. This term was coined around 35 years ago[21] but has recently gained prominence for tragic reasons. It describes the practice of peddling a supposedly sustainable agenda for the sake of appearing to care about the environment. It might even extend to intentionally deceiving consumers about the environmental impact of a certain product. It is inexcusable and no doubt one of the worst displays of short-termism and shareholder primacy. It is our duty to call this out vocally and visibly, and to shine a light only on the true champions of sustainability and environmentally responsible practices.

THE SECOND VIRTUE OF BUSHIDO: COURAGE

At first, this may seem simple and self-explanatory, but courage is a multifaceted concept. Courage should be purposeful. It should not take the form of bravery for the sake of bravery. Ego-fueled bravado and pomp have very little to do with courage; at most, they can be thought of as courage's distant relatives.

In today's businesses, courage helps leaders challenge the norms, question constantly and scrutinize indiscriminately.

Once again, courage is necessary to experiment and innovate, particularly under pressure. Being curious requires courage, and it is the courageous business leaders who swim against the tide and thereby achieve truly exceptional things.

In many senses, courage goes hand in hand with rectitude. Speaking up for what is right and what is wrong also requires immense courage. Business leaders today must be principled and unafraid of objecting vocally to practices that do not comply with either the letter or the spirit of law and regulation.

Whistleblowers are courageous. Calling out the misdeeds or misbehaviours of peers, and even colleagues who are more senior or more established within an organization, requires great courage. But truly courageous people are also able to hold themselves to account, practice self-criticism and admit to their shortcomings.

The times when I have had to muster the most courage have been when I have had to confess a weakness or an inability and seek help. Without courage, a leader cannot recognize their own failures or learn from their gravest mistakes or most flagrant trespasses.

Way back in 2006, the film *An Inconvenient Truth*[22] about Al Gore's mission to educate the populous on global warming showed us that our planet was getting precariously close to the breaking point. We are even closer now. As of the middle of 2020, the concentration of carbon dioxide in our atmosphere was the highest it had been in human history.[23] Between 1990 and 2016, to fuel our lifestyles and habits, the world lost around 502,000 square miles, or about 1.3 million square kilometers, of forest, which is roughly equivalent to the size of South Africa.[24]

We are consuming voraciously and insatiably, seemingly unconcerned about the ways in which our children and their children will suffer from the consequences of our recklessness. Greta Thunberg's warnings may be ringing in our ears but something, it seems, is still stopping us from taking decisive action.

WE MUST NOT LET THE PANDEMIC-INDUCED PAUSE ERASE PROGRESS.

___

WELLBEING

Other side effects of the Great Acceleration are still widely unaddressed, even considered taboo. The dominance of technology has created an always-on mentality across workplaces around the world. With global travel and communication easier than ever, a culture of presenteeism has spawned a mental health epidemic.

The American film director Woody Allen is widely quoted as having once said that 80% of success in life can be attributed to simply showing up,[25] but our obsession with showing up, even when we're sick or fatigued, has already caused severe damage.

Wellbeing is at the very heart of everything we do at Sompo and that is why, two years ago, we redesigned our brand to communicate this priority in an unequivocal way. Security, health and wellbeing are pillars of our operations, and we are entirely dedicated to ensuring that all our stakeholders are given the potential to enjoy not only the highest quality of life, but also – and it may sound a little morbid at first – the highest quality of death.

We tend to shy away from thinking about our ultimate demise. First, it is hard to imagine how we might pass, and it is also not particularly pleasant dwelling on the prospect of having to leave our loved ones behind. Yet death remains an undeniable inevitability.

Wellbeing means living a comfortable and fulfilling life, and that extends to death, which ideally should be swift, natural and painless rather than premature or brought about by an entirely preventable condition. In Japan, we refer to this concept as *Pin-Koro*, where *Pin* means living a long life, the final days of which are filled with joy and laugher, and *Koro* means eventually experiencing a swift death.

Shamefully, Japan has made headlines as employees literally work themselves to death – a phenomenon termed *Karoshi* – but it is a rampant problem in many countries and particularly large metropolitan cities.

In Japan, many companies have woken up to the severity of the problem and some have even started to implement creative solutions to incentivize people to take breaks and look after their health.[26] I am fearful that many of these measures might not go far enough.

In some industries, employees are being pressured to not only compete with their peers and rivals, but also with the spectre of automation. One study in 2019 predicted that tens of millions of existing jobs would be taken over by robots in the next few decades as technology becomes more sophisticated, effectively making people redundant.[27] Of course, technology also has the power to create new jobs, jobs that are as exciting as they are fulfilling. However, the transition to a digital-first economy and labour market represents a tectonic shift. Humans, undoubtedly creatures of habit, are averse to the unknown and instinctively unwilling to sample something unfamiliar.

It is, therefore, perhaps not surprising that we've never been more troubled, more anxious or more stressed. Even before the COVID-19 pandemic, an estimated 275 million people were suffering from anxiety disorders, representing about 4% of the global population.[28]

In 2018, ahead of the first global ministerial mental health summit in London, a seminal piece of research found that mental health disorders were on the rise in every single country in the world and could cost the global economy up to $16 trillion between 2010 and 2030 if not addressed adequately.[29]

While the Great Acceleration cannot be blamed for every case of a mental health illness, there are connections. What we can conclusively establish is that, over the last 20 years, as a complex cocktail of forces has changed and shaped the world we live in, rates of stress, anxiety and depression have rocketed.

WORKFORCE DEMOGRAPHIC

Finally, the last 20 years have pushed and challenged our understanding of what makes a business truly responsible, in an entirely new way. The noise created by the speeding up of processes and innovation has caused us as a business community to lose sight of what really matters.

Amid rising inequality, the climate crisis and a mental health epidemic, many business leaders have failed to appreciate the changing needs of the workforce and the responsibilities corporations have to look after their people.

With the focus on technology, it has become easy to forget that humans are the true machines that keep businesses running. We are the most important resource any business – regardless how automated – will ever have.

Many have neglected to appreciate the implications of an ageing workforce. This is a demographic trend my company, Sompo Holdings, is acutely aware of. In the 20 years to 2018, global life expectancy increased from about 67 years to 72.5 years.[30] Labour force participation rates in developed economies have risen for older people because of higher life expectancy and better education, but also because of financial concerns.

This trend, coupled with globalization and a digitalization of the workforce, has forced managers to perform a balancing act. The hunt to recruit tech-savvy individuals who are agile, curious and worldly is a priority. However, it is equally necessary to retain experienced members of the workforce who, despite potential aversion to adopting new skills, offer indispensable industry knowledge. The rush of everyday business, in the hustle to keep up with the Great Acceleration, disturbs this delicate balance.

THE LAST TWO DECADES HAVE UNEQUIVOCALLY DEMONSTRATED THAT CAPITALISM MUST BE REDEFINED TO BE SUSTAINABLE.

LESSONS TO LEARN

The Great Acceleration of the last two decades has undoubtedly enriched our world. Technology has helped us connect, share and explore widely. It has helped us make huge leaps in scientific discovery. In 2003, scientists sequenced the entire human genome,[31] significantly progressing disease treatment, and supporting our understanding of evolution and molecular medicine. Elsewhere, technology has delivered electric cars onto roads worldwide,[32] exerting intense pressure on traditional car manufacturers to pivot to survive.

But although all these achievements should be celebrated, they remain just one side of the story. The last two decades have demonstrated unequivocally that capitalism must be redefined in order to be sustainable. As business leaders, we can no longer blindly chase profits if that means exacerbating a raging climate crisis. We have a duty to help solve the deep and harrowing problems of inequality. We must be held accountable when it comes to the physical and mental health of our labour forces.

THE THIRD VIRTUE OF BUSHIDO: BENEVOLENCE

"Under the regime of feudalism, which could easily degenerate into militarism, it was benevolence that we owed our deliverance from despotism of the worst kind," wrote Nitobe in *Bushido: The Soul of Japan*. He emphasized that a man who has the power and constitution to kill in battle must also demonstrate mercy.

In today's workplace, and particularly considering the dynamics shaping the corporate world, this is perhaps best understood as empathy; as a duty of care and even a certain tenderness toward those within our communities.

It might also be understood as compassion. For decades, this has been a persona non-grata in offices and boardrooms around the world. Throughout the industrial revolutions I've referenced in this book, many societies have celebrated a culture of leadership characterized by fierceness and determination, resolve and grit, brash machismo and Machiavellian swagger. Strongmen have been applauded for their ability to take control. Any talk of emotion has been deemed inappropriate in the workplace.

But humans are inherently emotional. Suppressing our fear, our passion, our grief, our rage and even our love just because we are in a professional environment is tiring and unrealistic.

We are not robots, and we are thankfully not carbon copies of each other.

Business leaders must be comfortable enough with their authority to be able to recognize and acknowledge the moods, emotions and feelings of their workforces and to provide counsel and support. Being benevolent, empathetic and compassionate also means being able to listen and to understand – or to know when it's impossible to understand what someone might be going through.

Many business leaders are exceptionally skilled at voicing their own interests and concerns, or those of their organization, but a truly good communicator is somebody who can be still, listen and gauge what their employees really need.

We must also become better at recognizing opportunities to learn. The Great Financial Crisis of 2008 and 2009, for example, came about because of irrational exuberance[33] on an unprecedented scale. The risks associated with subprime mortgages paled in comparison to the potential of making huge financial gains. Similarly, the burst of the dot-com bubble happened because of immense speculation and misplaced optimism, not rooted in reality, but built on flimsy hopes. These episodes should have taught us humility, of practicing a version of capitalism based on reason and rationale, rather than short-sightedness and the dream of a quick win.

We must ask ourselves whether the way we measure success, gauge performance and growth is still relevant and appropriate or whether the yardsticks we use are actually antiquated and unreliable, and therefore part of the problem.

Many of the world's largest economies have, over the last century, shifted from being driven by manufacturing to being driven by services and intangibles. Data has become a commodity that is arguably unparalleled in value and yet we struggle to definitively establish how to measure it's value.

We are still overly reliant on gross domestic product as a metric of national prosperity, but its shortcomings are becoming more painfully evident all the time.

Academics, including Joseph Stiglitz, have repeatedly flagged that our economic yardsticks fail to account for factors like environmental degradation and resource depletion. In an article for *the Guardian* newspaper published in 2019, he asserted that, "If our economy seems to be growing but that growth is not sustainable because we are destroying the environment and using up scarce natural resources, our statistics should warn us." The reality is that they do not.[34]

Even way back in March 1968, during a speech at the University of Kansas, Robert Kennedy raised grave concerns about the use of gross national product as an indicator of domestic success:

> *Our Gross National Product, now, is over $800 billion dollars a year, but that Gross National Product – if we judge the United States of America by that – that Gross National Product counts air pollution and cigarette advertising, and ambulances to clear our highways of carnage. It counts special locks for our doors and the jails for the people who break them. It counts the destruction of the redwood and the loss of our natural wonder in chaotic sprawl.*

It counts napalm and counts nuclear warheads and armored cars for the police to fight the riots in our cities. It counts Whitman's rifle and Speck's knife, and the television programs that glorify violence to sell toys to our children. Yet the gross national product does not allow for the health of our children, the quality of their education or the joy of their play. It does not include the beauty of our poetry or the strength of our marriages, the intelligence of our public debate or the integrity of our public officials. It measures neither our wit nor our courage, neither our wisdom nor our learning, neither our compassion nor our devotion to our country, it measures everything, in short, except that which makes life worthwhile. And it can tell us everything about America except why we are proud that we are Americans.[35]

An old adage argues: what gets measured, gets done. Based on this truth, we need to overhaul the way we consider, assess and track our performance as countries. We need to do this to create accountability and to set specific targets and goals. A number that implies top level economic prosperity could easily disguise massive inequality and ruinous climate change. I suspect it might not capture and measure the true impact a pandemic has on a country.

Take heart. It is not too late to correct our course. We face an inflection point. On the heels of the Great Acceleration is a monumental Forced Pause. The repercussions of the global health crisis have already been extensive and its effects will continue to ripple through every aspect of life and business for years to come. This is a precious opportunity for us to reflect, rebuild and recalibrate. It is an opportunity we cannot afford to miss. There is too much at stake.

PART 1: SUMMARY

Since the turn of the century, the world has endured a period of immense acceleration that has led to brilliant advances in technology and healthcare, among other things, but that has also had unintended consequences. Inequality has been exacerbated, and an immense strain has been placed on our planet.

The workplace has changed dramatically, too, and as a result of our new hyperconnected world, stress and mental health issues have become more prevalent than ever before.

It is critical that we, as leaders, are aware not only of the advantages of the Great Acceleration, but also of the downsides. We must learn from these lessons if we want to ensure that our families and communities will have a bright and prosperous future.

PART 2

FORCED
PAUSE

On 8 January 2020, an inconspicuous news item claimed one small paragraph in the bottom left-hand corner of the front page of *The Wall Street Journal*: "Chinese scientists investigating a mystery illness that has sickened dozens in central China have discovered a new strain of coronavirus."[36] Few paid much attention. Elsewhere, parts of Asia were reeling from the consequences of protests in Hong Kong; diplomatic relations between the US and Iran dominated front pages around the world. In the UK, the BBC was running a story on whether planting trees really can mitigate the effects of climate change.

In subsequent weeks, as news reports emerged of outbreaks of the mysterious new disease in ski resorts and on cruise ships, it became apparent this obscure sickness would not quickly pass.

By March, the situation was grave. Concerned by the contagion of the virus and its severity, the World Health Organization characterized COVID-19 as a pandemic.[37] By that point, more than 118,000 cases in 114 countries had been recorded, leading to 4,291 deaths.

Few anticipated how quickly and dramatically the situation would escalate. On 4 March, the WHO reported that over one million cases had been confirmed worldwide, marking a more than tenfold increase in less than a month. Rates would increase exponentially and indiscriminately around the world, dealing immense blows to some of the world's biggest economies and healthcare systems. Huge proportions of the labour market were forced to work remotely, overhauling their routines and ways of living. In addition to the devastating impact the virus has had on individuals' physical health, it has also exacerbated the mental health crisis and widened inequality.

Unemployment rates skyrocketed, disproportionately affecting female workers and those who were already in low-paying or insecure jobs.[38] Economic inequality widened at a terrifying rate. Sofia Sprechmann, Secretary-General of humanitarian agency Care International, in July 2020 described COVID-19 as the biggest setback to gender equality in a decade,[39] echoing research conducted by consultancy McKinsey, which concluded that because of the coronavirus' "regressive effect on gender equality," global GDP growth could be $1 trillion lower in 2030 than it would be otherwise.[40]

Most recessions are caused by a demand shock, a supply shock or some kind of systemic financial shock, like the collapse of a major financial institution. COVID-19, however, has potentially created a mixture of all three.[41]

The newfound interconnected news of economies and industries – a product of the Great Acceleration – has had many upsides for communities around the world, but it has also made us far more vulnerable. I think of it as a domino chain that has become increasingly connected, increasingly complex, because of globalization. When everything works, our ever-more-sophisticated supply chains are wonderfully efficient. But if one domino falls, it is only a matter of time before the others tumble too.

THE FOURTH VIRTUE OF BUSHIDO: POLITENESS

Nitobe writes that "politeness is a poor virtue, if it is actuated only by a fear of offending good taste." Instead, he adds, "It should be the outward manifestation of a sympathetic regard for the feelings of others." In this sense, benevolence and politeness bind together and the latter might more often be referred to as respect.

As we seek to reconstruct a model of capitalism and business that is fit for the world we live in, and that is advantageous to every stakeholder, we must honour the fact that respect can never be conditional.

The greatest rivalries – be they professional, personal or even on the sports field – should always be anchored in mutual respect. Within any organization, the highest-ranking member of management should respect the lowest-paid staffer to precisely the same extent as they respect their equivalent.

As the chief executive of Sompo, this is a rule I never allow myself to break because I vividly remember how it feels to be on the lowest rung of the corporate ladder. I know it was politeness and respect that gave me the opportunities and resources to be where I am today. They not only ensured that I had the chance to prove myself, but they also gave me the confidence to realize my own worth.

Politeness is a trait many foreign tourists and travelers associate with Japan, almost to a comical extent. Exaggerated politeness has, over decades, fanned stereotypes about our nation that are not always entirely accurate. Stereotypes can, of course, be offensive and cause a host of other problems, but this is one that I have no real aversion to.

As even Nitobe acknowledges in his book, "There may be unnecessary niceties in ceremonious etiquette." But there's beauty to them, too.

Particularly in a world in which speed is glorified and multitasking is practiced as sport, isn't it wonderful we can still take time to greet each other with decorum, observe each other with patience and interact in a considered way? Social decorum must never be considered a waste of time or energy. I am proud of Japan's cultural proclivities and believe that – after the humour fades – others might also learn from them.

MY HOPE IS WE CAN LEARN LESSONS FROM THIS FORCED PAUSE.

———

OVERDUE REFLECTION

Imagine it is January 2020. Now ask any multinational business leader if they could halt all corporate travel or pivot to an entirely remote work set-up. Ask any medical professional or healthcare authority whether they could develop, approve and distribute a new vaccine in less than a year. Can you hear the laughter? And yet we managed to do all those things.

While these years will no doubt be recorded as an era of economic hardship and medical challenge, they will also be remembered as a period of great experimentation – and successful experimentation, at that. The Forced Pause gave us no choice but to push the parameters of what we believed to be feasible. It gave us an excuse to question why those parameters were there in the first place, and what it might take to shift them and achieve more.

It reminds me of media stories about people reflexively assuming superhuman strength to protect loved ones. In 2012, a 22-year-old woman made headlines in Virginia after she reportedly raised a BMW off her father after the car fell off a jack.[42] Some years earlier, local papers reported that a man in

Tucson, Arizona, had hoisted a Chevy Camaro off a trapped cyclist, potentially saving his life.[43] There is much research to be done into the phenomenon some academics have termed "hysterical strength," but I can't help but think of what we've witnessed since the outbreak of the pandemic as an example of it. We developed drugs and altered so much about our daily lives purely because we were left no other option. We did not realize how resilient and resourceful we were until we had no choice.

My hope is that we can truly internalize the lessons we have learned from this Forced Pause. To do so, we must first recognize what we have been taught.

THE FIFTH VIRTUE OF BUSHIDO: VERACITY

When it comes to defining the ideal leader, many will cite authenticity as a non-negotiable characteristic. While this concept is easy to reference, it is tough to define. Veracity, truthfulness and authenticity extend far beyond a commitment to not telling lies.

As all the other virtues of Bushido, this one relates to the others and perhaps most of all to courage. Demonstrating veracity – or being authentic – involves never exaggerating or underplaying your abilities to further self-interests. It means being brave enough to admit mistakes and to acknowledge limits.

Authentic leaders are those who can show weakness and ask for help. They act as a manager in a way consistent with the way they act as a friend, parent, child or spouse. Veracity means not putting on an act. It means doing away with airs and graces for the sake of winning support or currying favour. It means being polite and respectful for no other reason than it is right thing to do.

BUSINESS HAS THE POWER TO BE A FORCE FOR GOOD.

LEARNING TO PRIORITIZE

An overarching lesson from the pandemic is the importance of prioritizing. As global business ground to a necessary halt, we were all forced to take a long look in the metaphorical mirror and reconsider what we care about.

Much has been written about purpose in recent years, to the extent the word has taken on an unhelpful air of jargon. Every company seems to claim to be purpose-driven, without truly elaborating on what that means. But the pandemic has forced us to conjure up a definition. My hope is we can use this to guide us long after the sick have healed and the virus has been eradicated.

What I have concluded – and I hope others have, too – is that the ultimate goal of business, of commerce, and therefore of capitalism, should be to enhance the quality of all human lives in some way.

It is not an original argument. Philosophers, artists and some of the most renowned management experts have made it repeatedly and over centuries. Even Abraham Maslow's Hierarchy of Needs – one of the most widely studied and referenced psychological models – echoes it. Yet so many of today's most influential business leaders still seem blind to the importance of considering the basic needs and desires of the humans who work for them.

As the coronavirus spread, it quickly became apparent that business leaders who were ignoring health protocols in the interest of chasing economic gains were playing with fire. Agility and a willingness to do whatever it takes to protect and support all stakeholders was not just the ethically correct and responsible strategy, but also in many cases – and in the longer run – the more lucrative.

Companies and leaders who particularly earned respect and plaudits were the ones who pivoted aggressively and creatively. By mid-march 2020, as the severity of COVID-19 was starting to bite, many governments issued a call to industry to help deliver medical supplies and equipment.

In the weeks that followed, many companies pitched in, but LVMH was one of the first out of the starting blocks. Under the guidance of billionaire business tycoon Bernard Arnault, the luxury goods giant swiftly repurposed its factories. Instead of churning elaborately crafted perfume flasks off its production lines, it used its facilities to make plastic bottles of hand sanitizer.[44] These were rapidly distributed to hospitals around the country, where the number of infected patients was already increasing at an alarming rate. Later, LVMH also pledged to help address a surgical mask shortage. Similarly, Ford[45] and Airbus[46] used their vast resources and financial clout to help make critical equipment, like sanitizer, ventilators and masks.

These case studies demonstrate the extent to which business have the power to be a force for the general good, if they are willing and able to look beyond short-term profits and shareholders' immediate interests. They show us what is possible if corporations honour not just their legal duties, but also their moral and ethical duties within our shared ecosystem. Our goal now must be to normalize this practice. Business leaders must ask themselves, every day, what they can do to help the many while furthering their own goals. Being charitable and being profitable do not have to be mutually exclusive pursuits. It is rare, in fact, that they are.

SOMPO'S COVID-19 STRATEGY

In order to understand Sompo's COVID-19 strategy, it's important to understand a little about our history.

Although Sompo Holdings in its current form was borne out of a share exchange agreement between Sompo Japan Insurance and NIPPONKOA Insurance in October 2009, the roots of the business can be traced back much further – more than 130 years.

In 1888, the Tokyo Fire Insurance Company was established as Japan's first fire insurance company in response to a huge number of fires that regularly leveled significant areas of the city entirely. The fires were mostly caused by accidents – fire was used for cooking, heating and lighting in those days – but acts of arson weren't rare either. Meteorological conditions at the time also meant that Tokyo, or Edo as it was known at the time, was prone to dry weather and strong winds that could fan open flames and easily help them spread.

The formation of the Tokyo Fire Insurance Company was thus welcomed by the masses and, in 1893, a prominent Japanese entrepreneur called Zenjiro Yasuda absorbed the firm into a major financial conglomerate that he oversaw.

Half a century later, in 1944, Tokyo Fire Insurance, Imperial Marine Insurance, and First Engine & Boiler Insurance merged to become the Yasuda Fire & Marine Insurance Company, which eventually merged with Nissan Fire & Marine Insurance. Out of those enterprises, Sompo Japan was eventually created in 2002, followed by Sompo Holdings seven years later.

Right throughout its history, Sompo's mission has always been to contribute to the security, health and wellbeing of our customers and society as a whole, by providing insurance and related services of the highest quality possible. But in 2015, we decided to expand our horizons to really fulfil that goal.

Having previously focused almost exclusively on insurance, we decided in that year to expand our remit into the nursing care business. To truly honour our mission – our reasoning went – we need to be there for our clients before things turn bad, before they face a crisis or disaster for which they require support from an insurance company.

We truly believe that the nursing care sector is critical to the functioning of a healthy society and, as a major business with the capabilities to support that sector, we considered it our duty to do so.

Japan is a nation grappling with challenges related to an ageing society that other nations will, before long, have to contend with too. At Sompo, our nursing care business represents an investment in our future common good, and we're working hard to develop sustainable nursing care services that employ technologies and data to enable individuals to live as comfortably and happily as possible and in whatever way that they choose.

As COVID-19 started to claim lives and livelihoods, we found ourselves in a similar situation to many other businesses around the world. This was brand-new territory. There was no instruction manual to deal with a global pandemic. I repeatedly found myself unsure of what to do.

What I was certain of, however, was that our people were our priority and I, as a leader but also as a responsible citizen, would do everything within my power to protect and support them through this troubling period.

While the health and wellbeing of all our employees is of paramount importance, our people – particularly in the nursing business – had an essential job to do for the wider community.

During Japan's state of emergency, Sompo Care, the care business within the broader Sompo group, continued its business operations and we decided to pay a special allowance to our staff who were providing frontline services under immensely difficult conditions, often going so far as to put their own lives at risk. I was in awe of our staff's tremendous effort and their unwavering sense of mission to protect those who rely on them.

Across our insurance business, my instinct might have been to shut everything down as a matter of precaution. But our operations had to keep running. They are indispensable to our customers, and it is our duty to support our customers' needs, especially during difficult times.

We are agile. Sompo's management was quick to implement new and inventive ways of working to keep our employees safe while still allowing them to do their jobs. The crisis has been extremely disorientating for many. We communicated with our staff regularly and openly. We quickly understood the value of strong, clear communication, and emphasis on community, as a means of getting through some of the hardest days and nights.

When I look at political leaders, I believe the ones we should be championing as role models are those who demonstrated a deep sense of humanity when COVID-19 upended our daily lives. Politicians who excelled were those who led by example and tried to truly understand the lived experiences of the people they govern. The pandemic served as a litmus test and a means of determining which leaders truly care, and which simply act as if they do.

BEING CHARITABLE AND BEING PROFITABLE ARE NOT MUTUALLY EXCLUSIVE PURSUITS.

LIVING WITH UNCERTAINTY

One concept I have spoken of often in recent years is VUCA. The US Army War College adopted the acronym in the late 1990s to sum up an increasingly Volatile, Uncertain, Complex, and Ambiguous environment.[47] After the 9/11 terror attacks in New York City, the expression gained traction and it has since been used with increasing frequency.

The VUCA world is characterized by such developments as the Trump presidency in the US, Brexit, and a rise in populism across parts of Europe. What these things all have in common is they have forced us to question beliefs we'd previously considered unshakeable, and challenge norms we'd formerly accepted. The pandemic is yet another manifestation of the VUCA world. It reminds us nothing should ever be expected or taken for granted. Tokenism is once again entirely inadequate.

Many businesspeople around the world might have been fortunate enough to be surprised by catastrophe but, in Japan, many of us are still scarred by the events of 2011. On 11 March, just before 3pm local time, an earthquake occurred off the Pacific coast of Tohoku, a region of Honshu island. It devastated the country.

At the time, it was the fourth most powerful earthquake since record-keeping began and the most powerful ever to occur in Japan. It quite literally shifted the earth on its axis, killed almost 16,000 people and injured countless more.[48] A decade later, countless people who had been displaced by the quake were still living away from their homes.

The structural damage caused by the earthquake and resulting tsunami was colossal. Japan's prime minister at the time, Naoto Kan, said that in the 65 years since the end of World War II, this had been the toughest and most difficult crisis for Japan.[49]

For the common good of society, every Sompo employee helped and supported in any way they could. From the highest-ranking executive to the most recent graduate hire, no questions were asked. No one hid behind their day job or routine responsibilities. Everyone showed agility, courage, creativity and empathy, and channeled their energy into helping the masses. Just as many have in the face of the COVID-19 pandemic.

In years to come, we may well go through periods of calm. Global conflicts might abate. Breakthroughs in healthcare might provide hope of a safer world. Countries that are politically polarized might succeed in bringing opposing sides of the debate together, and natural disasters might not happen. But it will be during those times we must remember 2020 and 2021. We must remember what it felt like to be facing tumult and crisis with no certain guidance on what to do next.

For now, we should consider this time as our chance to start over and reinvent the parameters and ideals we want to live by. Opportunities like this are rare. We must cherish them and consider very carefully how to use them in the best possible way.

THE SIXTH VIRTUE OF BUSHIDO: HONOUR

All conscientious business leaders strive to be honourable, but few take the time to dwell on what it really means and how it is particularly relevant in today's complex world.

To me, being honourable encompasses many of the values we have already discussed. It relates to being polite and respectful, but also to being authentic and true. It has much to do with being dedicated to fairness and equality. Being honourable also involves being compassionate and empathetic: being human in whatever role we assume.

Etymologically, the word honour can be traced back to the Latin word *honos*,[50] which was used to describe esteem or repute, or to refer to concrete indications of that repute – ceremonies or awards, for example. In the Roman Republic and early Roman Empire, the expression *cursus honorum* was used to refer to a sequential order of public offices held by politicians and those aspiring to be political leaders. It conveyed the order of seniority of those roles and the prestige associated with each.

I believe it would be misleading for honour to be associated with seniority. Throughout my long career as a businessperson, I have observed embodiments of honour at every level of organizational hierarchies. Anyone can be as honourable as a

PART 2: FORCED PAUSE

CEO or chairperson. To be honourable simply means behaving and treating others in a way that is befitting of someone who cares about all the other values that Bushido comprises.

BUSINESS HAS THE POWER TO BE A FORCE FOR THE COMMON GOOD IF WE LOOK BEYOND SHORT-TERM PROFITS AND SHAREHOLDERS' IMMEDIATE INTERESTS.

PART 2: SUMMARY

The global pandemic forced almost every industry in the world to adjust and change quickly to adapt to an unforeseen challenge. Many businesses and systems had to pause entirely. It is critical that we recognize the opportunity in crisis and consider this pause to be a gift.

Business leaders should use the Forced Pause as a chance to reflect holistically on their wider role in society and not just within their organization. They should also use it as an opportunity to reconsider their priorities and ensure that they are prepared to deal with future shocks and bouts of uncertainty. Agility is an indispensable quality of a responsible and effective leader.

PART 3

RECALIBRATING CAPITALISM

In March 1992, while I was working for The Yasuda Fire and Marine Insurance Company, a forerunner of Sompo, I was asked to take on some work for the Asian Development Bank and was transferred to Manila in the Philippines.

I was assigned to work in the Bureau of Human Resource Budget as part of a multinational team from New Zealand, Korea, India, the Philippines, the United States, Germany and, of course, Japan. My Korean colleague and I were the only ones without a PhD but he, at least, was a certified accountant. I was 35 years old, almost 2,000 miles from home and felt entirely like a fish out of water. My German colleague was brimming with confidence, quick to inform us that he had a doctorate in macroeconomics. I was awestruck – a familiar feeling over the following weeks as I settled into my new surroundings. My counterparts were all inherently talented and ambitious, quick to assimilate to the new culture and eager to embrace absolutely any professional challenge that came their way. I found myself flailing to keep up and longing for a more familiar environment.

I had to endure a six-month probation, after which I was hoping to get hired full time by the Development Bank, but a few weeks before the end of that period, my manager pulled me aside and told me the unhappy news: I had failed to impress him and needed to work harder to prove my worth.

I was distraught. Despite my early struggles, I was confident that I had progressed and performed adequately. But my English skills were a problem. Though my spoken language skills were adequate, I was not able to communicate as fluently when writing. Unsure of what to do, I turned to a senior Japanese colleague for counsel. He had become a mentor to me in the months since I had been in Manila, and I admired his cosmopolitanism, a product of having taught in the US for 25 years. "If you don't have the skills they require you to have to hire you," he said in an unsympathetic tone, "there's nothing you can do."

His words stung. I will forever be thankful for the lesson I learned in that moment about dealing with defeat in a gracious manner, but it was what happened next that perhaps taught me an even more important lesson for life. Aware of the fact that I could probably use a little company and distraction after suffering such a bitter blow, he invited me out for a drink.

Later that evening, I met my mentor in a pub he had suggested, but I was rather surprised to find the chosen location was in a rundown part of town that did not feel entirely safe. We had an enjoyable evening, punctuated with plenty of drinks and flowing conversation, and it was already past midnight by the time he stood up and told me he was heading home to bed. Before I could ask him to help me find my bearings and at least point me in the direction of my own home (or better still, drop me off!) he was already out of the door, and I was left entirely to my own devices.

After a somewhat cumbersome search, I managed to locate a taxi without getting mugged, but I was still angry the next day when I turned up to the office. "Why did you just abandon me like that?" I challenged him. "The problem is," he explained, revealing his plan all along, "Japanese people tend to rely on others too readily."

I was shocked and offended but, as the words sunk in, I started to appreciate his sentiment. "Kids growing up in the US or the UK are constantly told to stand on their own two feet and think for themselves," he elaborated. "We in Japan are too often told what to do, which has conditioned us to always wait for instructions before actually doing what we think needs to be done." By abandoning me the previous night, he had certainly made me uncomfortable, but he was also showing me tough love. He was trying to tell me that I was far more independent and capable than I was giving myself credit for.

Today, decades on, and with the immense benefit of perspective and hindsight, I fully appreciate what my mentor taught me. Though I do not necessarily agree with his vast cultural generalizations about the Japanese, I passionately subscribe to the idea that so many of us too often underappreciate the power of our own initiative and how much we can achieve if we put our mind to it rather than waiting for directions or some kind of external impetus.

As I have hopefully demonstrated so far in this book, many of the systems by which we live and conduct business are broken. What we all must understand now is that nobody is going to provide us with a step-by-step manual to fix them. The responsibility falls to each of us individually. It is yours, too.

In this section of the book, I will examine what needs to be done to recalibrate capitalism and create a more sustainable and responsible framework for everything that we do. But, just as I ultimately had to brave the streets of downtown Manila alone, every one of us needs to understand the specific part that they themselves must play in fixing what is broken: we must stand on our own two feet to truly get this job done.

Pick up a pen. Make notes as you read this section. The recalibration of capitalism relies on you and we must work together.

CREATIVE DESTRUCTION

As I write, we are still in the throes of the global coronavirus pandemic. Though some countries, through strict public health policies and preemptive action, have been able to control the spread or even eliminate the virus entirely, others have acted too late and are paying the price.

As of the start of 2021, more than 90 million cases of COVID-19 had been confirmed worldwide, and almost 2 million deaths,[51] though the real toll may never be known. It is hard amid battle to adopt a long-term perspective – to consider anything beyond the immediate horizon – but it is imperative that we do so. As we emerge from this health crisis – and we will – it is important we don't waste the opportunity to rebuild intelligently, to recalibrate capitalism in a responsible way.

In 1942, Austrian economist Joseph Schumpeter coined the term *Creative Destruction* to argue that change happens more swiftly and creatively during periods of economic disruption. He argued that technologies and processes are constantly revolutionizing the economic structures that determine the way we live, from within. They are "incessantly destroying the old one, incessantly creating a new one," Schumpeter wrote in his book, *Capitalism, Socialism and Democracy.*[52]

Over the decades, much evidence has emerged to support Schumpeter's theory. Henry Ford's automobile production line is widely cited as a prime example of creative destruction, but recent examples exist too. Academics and commentators have frequently drawn on Schumpeter to explain why highly innovative businesses often spring up in the aftermath of economic crises.

But as new businesses flourish after an economically difficult time, so too can new ideals, new visions and new standards.

Having survived a sudden Forced Pause after such a prolonged period of intense acceleration, and having witnessed how much can be achieved when under immense pressure, we should be brave enough to question the fundamental parameters of capitalism. We should determine what is truly important and what our objectives really are, in everything that we do.

Our natural world is the most precious commodity that we share. It is not sufficient – and never was – to treat sustainability as an afterthought. Considerations about the environment should permeate everything we do, as leaders, employees and responsible citizens. We must understand that fragility of our ecosystem and the extent to which we have already inflicted an immense amount of damage. It is now our duty to fix our predecessors' mistakes and to safeguard our successors' basic right of being able to live in a safe and healthy world.

TAKE THE
LONG-TERM VIEW

Arguably, one of the great shortcomings of present-day cap-italism has been an excessive focus on the short-term and on immediate gains. In the field of behavioural economics, present bias describes the human habit of valuing instant gratification over future satisfaction.[53] It is not something we should blame ourselves for; it is a characteristic that is deeply ingrained in our psychology. But to be responsible business leaders and citizens, it is something we must be aware of, particularly when we make decisions with important implications for our stakeholders.

Throughout my life, I have observed the downsides of short-ter-mism time and time again. I've seen CEOs making decisions intended to bring about long-term prosperity for stakeholders, but then changing course swiftly if they don't yield immediate results. Time, energy and money are wasted simply because executives aren't patient enough.

In business, people want to be able to show their shareholders quick quarter-by-quarter gains. Many business decisions that would be of immense benefit to a particular organization are not implemented because those responsible for the hard work will not be around to take credit for their gains when they come to fruition.

Similarly, I have seen corporate boards fire executives because they feel compelled to have a scapegoat – to find someone to blame for a short-term downturn in business or a temporary headwind. This comes back to a cultural misunderstanding of what makes a good leader: leadership quality should never be determined by how ruthless someone can be when it comes to placing blame. It should never be determined by how aggressive or bold a top-down decision is. Instead, it should be determined over a long period of time and based on a whole spectrum of metrics, most of which relate back to the values of Bushido.

At Sompo, we try to avoid the pitfalls and temptations of short-termism by first being acutely aware of them. We understand it is human nature to be inherently motivated by our own achievements and accompanying recognition, and we know it is instinctive to focus on achieving victories that we can quickly claim as our own.

So, we gently encourage employees to overcome these natural intuitions by educating them and create incentives for behaviours to change. If short-termism continues to dominate the way corporations are run, this year's revenues and profits will always be of greater importance than the impact the product line might have on the environment over the next five or ten years. It will always be more important to safeguard shareholders' dividends or bosses' end-of-year bonuses than to spend money on ensuring a solid pipeline of talent for years to come.

The truth, however, is that many businesses are unaware of how much this attitude costs and to what extent it is exposing them to risks. The long-term sooner-or-later always becomes the short term. If actions are not taken now to reduce carbon footprints, offer products and services in a more sustainable way, and ultimately stop climate change in its tracks, the effects will be felt in many years to come, but also immediately.

I believe in capitalism. I understand that money talks. I am also aware of human nature, and what motivates us to do what we do. I believe we should leverage this intelligently. If humans are encouraged by financial gains, then we must create financial incentives to encourage actions that might not be immediate. We need to do whatever it takes to expand horizons and to create an awareness of the knock-on effect of everything we do. Our mistakes now will be the problems of future generations. It is our responsibility to solve the problems we create.

THE SEVENTH VIRTUE OF BUSHIDO: LOYALTY

The seventh virtue of the Samurai described in Nitobe's book is loyalty. Again, it is necessary to dig below the surface to understand the essence and ethos of this virtue and to appreciate how it can help guide us as responsible business leaders.

In many ways, loyalty relates to some of the concepts that I addressed earlier on in this book. It means subscribing to the broader mission and stated purpose of a business or organization. This is where multi-stakeholder capitalism should come into its own. As the CEO of Sompo, I am as loyal to my shareholders as I am to any other of Sompo's stakeholders. I consider it my ironclad duty and responsibility to support the interests of anyone and everyone who is in the broader Sompo ecosystem. That includes members of the community in which our businesses operate. It includes the families of the people who work for us, who give their time and energy to our business. It includes our suppliers and customers, and it includes our partners.

What is often missed is that being truly loyal to all stakeholders means also considering the future.

This is where the problematically entrenched habit of short-termism becomes relevant. If, as a CEO, I am not considering the environmental impact of my company's actions, then I am not being loyal to my future stakeholders, who will be forced to live with the consequences.

Loyalty means being committed to the best interests of every stakeholder today, tomorrow and in years to come, and even, when necessary, putting their interests ahead of my own. Related to this, and in addition to my role as CEO of Sompo, I serve as the chair of Keizai Doyukai, the Japan Association of Corporate Executives, which is one of this country's leading business associations.

In 2020, Keizai Doyukai launched a forum dedicated to dialogue, which we called the "Future Selection Forum," where all different types of stakeholders, including future generations, are encouraged to discuss and debate current problems and possible solutions for a more sustainable Japan.

The motivation behind this forum is to encourage people to consider the future and think for the longer term, rather than stay focused on the present.

AS NEW BUSINESSES FLOURISH AFTER AN ECONOMICALLY DIFFICULT TIME, SO TOO CAN NEW IDEALS, NEW VISIONS AND NEW STANDARDS.

ABOLISH SHAREHOLDER PRIMACY

It is more important than ever that businesses move away from a system of shareholder primacy and for leaders to come down on the right side of the shareholder-versus-stakeholder debate that has been raging for years and has frequently pitted the East versus the West.

In September 1970, economist Milton Friedman penned an article in *The New York Times*[54] that defined an entire age of capitalism. Under the title "The Social Responsibility of Business Is to Increase its Profits," Friedman argued precisely that. He described businesspeople who claim that a corporation's goal should be to promote "social" ends as "unwitting puppets of the intellectual forces" and accused them of "undermining the basis of a free society." The "social responsibilities of business," demonstrated "analytical looseness and lack of rigor," he continued, stipulating that "only people can have responsibilities."

Many individuals whom I have encountered throughout my career, at Sompo and elsewhere, would no doubt be quick to counter this Friedman doctrine. And yet evidence of real action is still lacking. Once again, tokenism raises its ugly head.

There is evidence we are moving in the right direction. In August 2019, the Business Roundtable, a group widely considered to comprise the CEOs of the US's largest and most influential corporations, committed publicly to abandoning the attitude that maximizing shareholder value should be a company's primary objective.[55]

A joint statement by the members announced that the interests of the owners of shares in their companies would no longer automatically take precedence over the interests of other stakeholders, like clients, employees and suppliers. They also explicitly committed to respecting the people in the communities in which their businesses operate, and the environment, "by embracing sustainable practices across our businesses."

A few months later, in his annual letter to BlackRock shareholders,[56] the chief executive of the asset management bellwether, Larry Fink, committed to "place sustainability at the center of [BlackRock's] investment approach."

Although his company was not going to divest of companies in its index funds, the CEO warned that BlackRock would be "increasingly disposed to vote against management and board directors when companies are not making sufficient progress on sustainability-related disclosures and the business practices and plans underlying them."

These are encouraging signs of a growing awareness of the risks associated with shareholder primacy. But much more still needs to be done.

I believe we can use the forces of capitalism, and the dynamics of human nature, to bring about real change. We need to create transparency and accountability by introducing measurable goals that set standards. Shareholder primacy is one of the ugliest and most destructive facets of the old-school version of capitalism from which we must move on. Promoting a dialogue is, of course, a first necessary step, but we should have progressed far beyond that by now and should already be engaging in real, tangible action.

TREAT HUMANS AS HUMANS

Milton Friedman also claims a business cannot hold responsibilities because only humans can have responsibilities. To my mind, this logic is flawed, quite simply because businesses are humans.

As corporations have evolved and adapted to new challenges, embraced automation and the newly competitive forces of the globalized world, the human importance of a company has too often been trivialized – even forgotten. Automation has made many roles previously performed by humans redundant, but the need for emotional intelligence in a workforce – for judgment, argument and social skills – has perhaps never been greater.

HUMAN-CENTRIC TECHNOLOGY AT SOMPO

The industries in which Sompo operates are ideal candidates for technological innovation. Amid all the hype, however, it is critical that our teams always remember the overarching mission of Sompo: to enhance security, health and wellbeing during life and into death. In pursuit of this goal, we are always searching for new ideas, entities and partners. To do this, we have created a dedicated subsidiary whose goal it is to bring together pioneering startups with established players within and beyond the broader insurance industry.

Today, we have locations in several technology hubs around the world – Silicon Valley, Tel Aviv, as well as Tokyo – which has given us unique access to budding enterprises where we see great potential.

In 2017, for example, we helped a Taiwan-headquartered company called Health2Sync with its Series B funding round because we were deeply impressed by the diabetes tracking technology the team had developed.

In recent years, we have also collaborated with two Israeli startups that we're particularly excited about. One, called Medigate, is developing cyber security solutions for health-care organizations to ensure that patient data is never compromised. The second, binah.ai, offers a mobile application for users to manage their stress levels wherever they are and whatever they might be doing.

I feel both deeply excited and profoundly honoured to be a part of these startups' journeys, and I believe that our ability to collaborate with them for the common good of society is a perfect example of the virtues of the Bushido in action.

As we advance into an age defined by what World Economic Forum founder Klaus Schwab called the Fourth Industrial Revolution,[57] we must also be aware of the importance of skills and how these should be balanced and fostered. Over the last decade, STEM skills – those relating to science, technology, engineering and maths – have been celebrated as indispensable for being equipped to face an increasingly digital world. But let's think again.

Youngsters are often encouraged to study STEM subjects, rather than liberal arts or the humanities, because of the superior economic value they are thought to be able to generate. Financiers, scientists and engineers, so the theory goes, quite simply contribute more to the economy than artists, philosophers and historians.

This narrative has had a huge impact on shaping education systems around the world. In the US, for example, almost every field of humanities has seen a considerable drop in college majors in recent years.[58] The trend is also evident around the world.

Our reasons for encouraging the pursuit of STEM subjects are inherently flawed. Of course, STEM skills are important to navigate the future world of work, particularly as technological innovation accelerates. But to leverage the full potential of our STEM skills, we urgently need other skills – literacy, reasoning, interpretation and creativity.

Regardless of the extent to which automation overhauls workforces and transforms industries, emotional intelligence and other core transferable skills, honed by studying non-STEM subjects and especially philosophy, will always be necessary. This is particularly important as we navigate an increasingly polarized world, and wrestle to preserve cohesion and order in hyper-diverse societies. It is deeply important to understand humans in terms beyond facts and figures.

As two Canadian academics, Alan Sears and Penney Clark, succinctly argued in an article published in September 2020: "If the study of history, society, culture or the arts dies, our societies may learn the hard way that it takes more than narrow job preparation to ensure that our students will flourish as human beings. Such flourishing includes the willingness and ability to engage with the challenging and urgent social, cultural, environmental and political issues with which they are confronted in these times."[59]

SELF-CONTROL IN BUSHIDO

A final overarching notion that Nitobe emphasizes as part of Bushido is self-control. In his words, self-control "was universally required of Samurai." Nitobe characterized this trait as "calmness of behaviour" and "composure of mind" and argued these should not be "disturbed by passion of any kind."

Again, this essential trait must be adapted to be relevant for today's working environment. The constant refrain that I keep returning to throughout this book is that we are all humans and our emotions and feelings are the colours that make us unique, that make life exciting, enriching and rewarding. To quash our emotions is to deny ourselves a basic pleasure. We should embrace them and celebrate them, and we should understand that bottling them up, can strain on our health.

But that is not to say we should allow ourselves to indulge in emotional outbursts whenever we feel the urge. As responsible individuals, we must understand the repercussions of everything we do and say. As a manager, this is especially important.

In 1936, Dale Carnegie, an American lecturer, published *How to Win Friends and Influence People*.[60] Carnegie wrote the book after a businessman, working for the publishing company Simon and Schuster, took a class that Carnegie was teaching on the importance of interpersonal skills when conducting business.

A mere 5,000 copies of the book were printed initially, but demand was rampant and, within the first year, 17 editions of the book had to be printed in order to keep sellers satisfied. It seemed that the business community had never seriously considered the potential commercial benefit of treating a client or partner with true respect, compassion and empathy. Up until this point, business transactions had been an unemotional domain: no place for feelings. But Carnegie's book, which subsequently went on to be considered one of the most influential business books of all time, fundamentally challenged that. By 2011 – the book's 75th anniversary – it had reportedly sold more than 30 million copies[61] and, even today, almost 85 years after first hitting shelves, *How to Win Friends and Influence People* is considered an invaluable guide by world-class negotiators and managers.

The core messages of the book, however, are hardly revelatory: be interested in your counterpart, show enthusiasm and smile, listen to what they have to say, speak to their interests, make them feel important and ensure that you are at least appearing authentic all the time. It is about self-control. It is about understanding how you are perceived by others and what impact you are having on others: how your actions are making them feel about themselves.

There is no art to it. It is simply self-awareness and what we now term *emotional intelligence*.

LEAD BY EXAMPLE

Although cultural change must eventually permeate every seniority level of an organization to be truly sustainable, the onus should at least initially fall on leaders to set an example to follow.

Countless books have been written about leadership, and yet it is a topic that is still frequently misunderstood. While many of us have no problem calling out – or even ridiculing – a misstep or a public faux pas, the qualities and traits that make a truly great leader often go unacknowledged. It is these, however, we must examine.

As the chief executive of a very large company, I appreciate it is my responsibility to take the initiative and to make decisions, as well as to counsel and guide. But I am also the first to admit that I am a simple man. I would not be able to speak of professional success if it were not for the people around me. I am as aware of the limits to my intellectual capacity, as I am of my talents and skills. I am unafraid of seeking help, and I am fully aware my judgment can err. I often make mistakes. But this attitude is an asset. Many executives, and even world leaders, do not reveal flaws or fallibility out of fear that it could make them look incompetent. I believe the opposite is true.

There are many leaders – historical and current – whom I admire and endeavour to emulate. During different phases of my life, I have had different role models, but one person I have consistently looked up to is the late Kōnosuke Matsushita, who founded Panasonic.

THE LIFE AND LEGACY OF KŌNOSUKE MATSUSHITA

Matsushita was born in 1894 in Wakayama Prefecture in Honshu. He was the youngest of eight children and lived comfortably until his father lost much of the family's wealth when a bet on the commodity market backfired. To support his family, young Matsushita, who was not yet out of elementary school, started earning a wage from an apprenticeship at a store in Osaka that made hibachi charcoal heaters. When that shop went out of business, he found work selling bicycles under a manager who particularly valued his entrepreneurial instincts and discipline.

Several years later, in the early 1900s, just as streetcars were starting to appear across the city of Osaka, Matsushita sensed the promise held by the fledging electronics industry. It was an exciting time and the dawn of a new industrial era. The teenager decided to apply for a job at the Osaka Electric Light Company. The work was treacherous. While wiring a major theatre, he suffered through a fierce bout of pneumonia, but his ambition and diligence paid off, and he was swiftly promoted through the corporate ranks.

At the age of just 22, Matsushita was promoted to inspector, which at the time was the highest position a technician could secure, but he was also frustrated. He was trying desperately to convince his supervisor of the merits of a new electrical socket that he had designed and built in his spare time. Uninspired and unchallenged by his day job, he could not stop thinking about the socket and the ways in which it might transform the market for electric appliances. In June 1917, after mustering up all his entrepreneurial spirit, he decided to leave his stable and decent-paying job and cast out on his own.

The decision involved a healthy portion of risk. Matsushita's savings did not even amount to 100 yen. But unperturbed by a dire lack of resources, he set up shop in a tiny apartment and got to work with the help of two former coworkers whom he had managed to lure from the Osaka Electric Light Company, as well as his wife's youngest brother.

The enterprise got off to a rocky start. Demand for the new socket failed to materialize and his two former colleagues quit the business before the year was out. The company was pushed to the very brink of bankruptcy before it even had a chance to truly establish itself, but Matsushita's self-belief and resolve were unrelenting and paid off. One day, seemingly out of the blue, he received an order for a thousand insulator plates for electric fans.

Slowly but surely other orders trickled in, fortifying the foundations of the business, now called Matsushita Electric Housewares Manufacturing Works. The growing team of workers started developing new products, including a two-way socket. By 1922, Matsushita had to build a new factory and office to accommodate the now-thriving company. Later he experimented with battery-powered bicycle lamps, affordable irons and then radios, all of which attracted floods of orders and raised the business profile nationwide.

As Matsushita thrived professionally, he started to consider the broader purpose of both his company and of manufacturers more generally. He reflected on religion and spirituality and is quoted as having said that while "religion guides people out of suffering toward happiness and peace of mind," business can similarly "contribute by providing physical necessities required for happiness." In fact, he concluded, "This should be its primary mission."[62]

In May 1932, he gathered all his employees and announced the introduction of an explicit corporate mission that all should commit to and abide by. An excerpt from that speech went as follows.

> The mission of a manufacturer is to overcome poverty by producing an abundant supply of goods. Even though water can be considered a product, no one objects if a passerby drinks from a roadside tap. That is because the supply of water is plentiful and its price is low. Our mission as a manufacturer is to create material abundance by providing goods as plentifully and inexpensively as tap water. This is how we can banish poverty, bring happiness to people's lives, and make this world a better place."[63]

In the subsequent years, Matsushita ensured that this mission and a broader ethos, which he summed up with the phrase "business is people," continued to resonate through each division and every seniority level of the company. He opened an employee training institute and, in August 1935, incorporated the company's trade department as the Matsushita Electric Trading Company.

In 1937, the Second Sino-Japanese War broke out, putting Matsushita's principles to the test. As Japan's economy faced pressure to militarize, the chief executive called on his employees to honour the values that he championed and that the business mission statement conveyed. To a large extent this worked, but the economic cost of the war was debilitating, and the company was forced to rebuild many factories and facilities from scratch as peacetime dawned.

Amid all these setbacks and challenges, it would have been easy for Matsushita to lose sight of his and his business's purpose, but he didn't. It would have been simple for him to give up on his pursuit of running an international corporation and providing meaningful jobs to hundreds of people, but he didn't. Instead, he reaped the benefits of his resilience and ethical disposition. After the war, as Japan battled ruinous inflation, Matsushita launched the PHP Institute, named for the concept of "Peace and Happiness through Prosperity," and dedicated to the interests of humans and human wellbeing in a work environment.

In 1961, after years of international success and expansion with brand names that included Panasonic, Matsushita stepped down as president of the company and was succeeded by his son-in-law. He retired in 1973 and passed away in 1989. But more than 100 years after taking that bold first step, his legacy lives on.

Panasonic is unequivocally one of the most important technology companies in the world today. As of March 2020, it employed over 250,000 individuals worldwide across hundreds of subsidiaries. The pandemic dealt a fierce blow to the company's performance, but it remains an industrial linchpin as a supplier to dozens of industries. While many factors have contributed to its durability and success, I am certain the Panasonic story would read very differently if it hadn't been for Matsushita's courage to innovate, willingness to take risks, and determination to always put people right at the very heart of business.

At its core, Matsushita's life – in the office, at home and on factory floors – was, in my opinion, driven by the virtues of Bushido. Though he endured periods of economic hardship and struggle, he never lost sight of his broader purpose as a businessman. He was brave and courageous, but not short-sighted or ego-driven. He was respectful, honest and honourable, while consistently understanding how to run a company in a fair way to provide equal opportunities to all.

There is no blueprint for what makes a good leader. This is the challenge. While Matsushita's life and career will never be emulated by anyone – his values, principles and beliefs certainly can.

He has served as a great inspiration to me throughout my long career so far, and I would encourage you to consider your own version of my Matsushita. Whose values do you admire? Who do you consider to be principled and purpose-driven in the very true sense of that phrase? Consider that person careful, study how they face the everyday challenges of corporate life. Then, define your own path forward.

A POSTSCRIPT ON BUSHIDO

Nitobe's principles of Bushido are flawed in many ways. They are geared toward a world that predates even the genesis of the Great Acceleration. They are misguided in their perception of gender and the roles that women and men should play in society. As business leaders, we are not warriors, and we should never glorify the roles we have beyond the responsibilities that define them. We should not mythologize our lives, and we shouldn't reside in the past.

But the underlying values that form the basis of Nitobe's book can create a foundation for our missions as leaders.

We must aspire to promote unconditional equality and be courageous in everything that we do. We must be kind and compassionate, honest and truthful. We must be authentic and honourable, by almost any definition of that term. We must understand whom we have a duty to be loyal to, and why that is the case, and we must always understand our power over others and exercise self-control accordingly. The essence of Bushido may date back centuries, but if we mold and shape it, it's relevance will never fade.

THE NEED FOR EMOTIONAL INTELLIGENCE IN A WORKFORCE — FOR JUDGMENT, ARGUMENT AND SOCIAL SKILLS — HAS NEVER BEEN GREATER.

PART 3: SUMMARY

We should consider it a privilege to have the chance to recalibrate the systems we live and work by as a result of the destruction caused by COVID-19. As we begin to rebuild, there are certain principles we should think about. We should ensure that we're taking the long-term view. Future generations will have to live with the consequences of the decisions we make today.

We must manage for the sake of the common good: shareholder primacy must be stamped out if we want to create a truly sustainable, happy and healthy world. And strong leadership is critical. Managers must create the businesses that they would want to work, regardless of the role. Strong communication, honesty, authenticity and fairness are all entirely indispensable.

PART 4

A BUSHIDO MANIFESTO

One of the most significant hurdles I have experienced so far when trying to effect change – either in myself, my team, my business or within the broader community – is that humans are creatures of habit. We are inherently driven by a familiarity bias that encourages us to default to doing things the way we have always done them. Though we might not know it, we tend to be a little afraid of change, or at least apprehensive. We are primed to shun the unfamiliar. Who can blame us? Centuries ago, this instinct probably saved our lives several times a day.

But things have changed and the systems we are using and the parameters we have established are no longer fit for purpose. We must find the courage for overhaul, even if that means embracing the great unknown.

To make the prospect more palatable, it is important we break down our vision into manageable steps and specifics tasks.

Anyone who has ever picked up a management handbook will understand the importance of creating specific, measurable and realistic goals for achieving success. We must apply this approach here. If we set ourselves the task of entirely overhauling capitalism, we are likely to be intimidated to the point of paralysis. Let us start ambitiously but realistically so that we can work systemically and determinedly.

WE MUST FIND THE COURAGE FOR OVERHAUL, EVEN IF THAT MEANS EMBRACING THE GREAT UNKNOWN.

COLLABORATION OVER COMPETITION

First, the importance and value of collaboration can't be underestimated.

Against the backdrop of the global pandemic, leaders from across business, politics, academia and beyond have all tried to sketch out ways in which we can create a system that is more responsible, sustainable and ethical.

In the world of business, we are often taught to engage fiercely in competition: to be the first and to be the best. Because of the way that markets work, I understand rivalry will always be a feature of the free economy. But that does not mean it's not important for all of us to appreciate the potential of collaboration and understand that in some situations – such as a global health crisis – collaboration is essential. If we respect each other's strengths and see each other as resources, we can achieve remarkable things. To be driven by self-interest is inherently dangerous.

To recalibrate capitalism in a way that will benefit the many rather than the few, we must be open to diverse perspectives and be prepared to draw on the knowledge and insights of experts from our global industries.

World Economic Forum founder Klaus Schwab notes in his book, *Stakeholder Capitalism*, published in January 2021, that within months of the pandemic beginning, work had already started on developing and bringing to market more than 200 potential vaccines. Progress was only made possible through cooperation: multinational companies partnered with public and private organizations. In addition to the examples I referred to in the second part of the book, AstraZeneca joined forces with Oxford University in the UK. Elsewhere, Schwab notes that companies like Unilever approached the WEF's COVID-19 Action Platform to offer support by providing hygiene products or ventilators.[64]

Schwab acknowledges it is certainly not rare for humans to act on virtuous instincts during times that are particularly hard or challenging, but the new form of capitalism we're working toward should normalize this sort of behaviour. Every employee, inspired by their manager, should consider how they can perform their professional duties in a way that helps the wider community and stakeholders – not just shareholders.

CELEBRATE VALUE AND ACHIEVEMENTS EVERYWHERE

The global pandemic has caused all of us to shift our perspectives in terms of what matters, what we care about and what's essential. Prior to 2020, few of us would have even bothered to acknowledge the privilege associated with being able to leave our apartments and walk down the street, breathing fresh oxygen, entirely unconcerned about our health and safety. Humans tend to suffer from short-term memory, so I suspect we will forget what it was like to be quarantined or locked down, and we will once again take our mundane civil liberties for granted. As business leaders, though, let's be better than that.

One very encouraging side effect of the pandemic has been that we have changed our collective perception of the people whose work it is to keep our societies functioning. Before COVID-19 hit, many of us will have taken for granted supermarket cashiers, bus drivers, delivery workers and even some healthcare workers, whose contribution to our society has always been vital to its survival. We now have a greater understanding, appreciation and respect for their contribution.

As our towns and cities ground to a sudden halt in the early months of 2020, we quickly understood that these people are entirely essential. As the pandemic raged, they tirelessly ensured that we had access to food and that we could travel to urgent hospital and doctor appointments. In many countries around the world, campaigns were organized to show appreciation for these employees, but my true hope is that this appreciation will not fade.

As business leaders, the lesson we should take from this pandemic is that every single person within our organization should be valued, championed and rewarded for the efforts they make and the challenges they overcome. Often, administrative staff, care workers and other individuals who work behind the scenes are forgotten about by those operating at the higher echelons of a company. This must not happen. They provide the backbone of businesses. They are essential and indispensable, and it is our duty to ensure that they understand how deeply they are appreciated for all that they do.

A final note here on the value of multigenerational workforces. The working population in many countries is getting older as individuals are being forced to stay employed for longer in order to live comfortably into retirement. Accommodating many generations within single teams is no doubt challenging. Skills and attitudes will differ from generation to generation, as might the underlying culture. But once again, mastering collaboration here can be immensely advantageous. Without threat or intimidation, we can all learn from each other. Hierarchies should not necessarily be dictated by age, but it's critical that everyone understands and respects each person's roles and responsibilities. Open communication should be encouraged and facilitated at all times, and transparency is key. We must also remember that this relates to diversity, too. As workforces that are more diverse in terms of race and gender tend to be more productive, so too do workforces that can show demographic diversity.

Perhaps on account of the media, we've developed a habit of using stereotypes and generalizing terms to refer to particular age groups: Boomers, Millennials and Generation X, for example. But here I would urge you to refrain from reducing any single person to such a label. Our aim should be to bridge generational gaps, foster intergenerational relationships and celebrate collaboration. Labels that might alienate or cement any real or perceived divisions might quickly thwart those noble intentions.

WE CAN ACHIEVE REMARKABLE THINGS.

_____

TAKE EVERY OPPORTUNITY TO SET AN EXAMPLE

When it comes to living life – or indeed conducting business – in a more sustainable way, it can be easy to fall into a trap of thinking that our small gestures and individual habits will not make an impact: "Recycling my coffee cup or plastic bag won't significantly exacerbate the climate crisis." This is dangerous thinking, particularly as a business leader. Anyone reading this book is fortunate enough to have some privilege and with that privilege comes a responsibility to set an example. Whether it is our intention or not, our actions set a standard for those who see us and provide a model that will be emulated.

What we do and the way we live must align with our understanding of what is responsible, what is ethical and what is sustainable.

This should extend across every part of business. We must all be champions of equality and diversity, and we must do whatever is within our power to ensure that an equality of opportunity exists within our communities. This relates directly back to many of the values of Bushido. Justice and courage are the most obvious: as leaders, we must never tolerate discrimination or bias, and we must be brave enough to call it out and to demonstrate that doing so is the right thing. But the other values are relevant here, too. True diversity within a workforce can only be achieved if no one feels undermined or belittled. Benevolence and politeness are critical. Veracity, or authenticity, are necessary, too. We need to be authentic to encourage others to be authentic and for them to understand that they will be accepted regardless of what they look like and where they come from.

I was encouraged when the Business Roundtable in the US committed publicly to abandoning profit maximization as the overriding goal of a corporation. But I also had concerns. Many of the executives who belong to that esteemed group earn huge paychecks – multiples of the average annual wages their employees take home. Many of them still succumb to the temptation of short-termism and some still convey the message that success can be measured in dollars alone. On account of their stratospheric success as heads of some of the world's most influential corporations, these CEOs are rarely challenged. That must change, too. We must hold executives, particularly the most visible and influential, to account. Greta Thunberg led by example; we must now be brave enough join her in her fight.[65] Although her generation brings with it great promise, we can't use that as an excuse to absolve ourselves of responsibility. In fact, we have a serious transitional responsibility. It is our duty to create the conditions for the potential aspirations of the next generation to flourish.

THINK BIG

Mariana Mazzucato, a professor at University College London, is a prolific writer and leading economist and her book, *Mission Economy*,[66] published in January 2021, aligns with many of the concepts, ideas and goals that I subscribe to.

Mazzucato contests that capitalism is in crisis. She examines the widening wealth gap and warns that the consequences will be dire if we fail to do something about it. She also highlights the extent to which we are wrecking the planet and emphasizes the need for a radical rethink of capitalism.

Her conjecture is that to solve big problems we must think big. We must understand the systemic nature of the issues that are threatening our future, and how they fit together. To create a better world, she argues, we must mobilize our resources in a way that is as creative, bold and innovative as the way in which we approached the first moon landing. Like Schwab, she also emphasizes the importance of collaboration across stakeholders. It is not enough just for corporations to work together: governments and agencies, both on a national and supranational level, must team up to in order to attain our common goals.

Globalization has earned, in recent decades, a reputation for being dangerously polarizing. Indeed, politicians like Donald Trump have, within the last 10 years, secured power off the back of campaigns that are rooted in the argument that globalization is a threat to sovereignty, has eroded national identity and even independence. This is something that both upsets and scares me. National borders serve an important purpose, but we should never wish for them to become diplomatic battlefronts the way that some of our world leaders want them to be. Isolationism is a dangerous premise and, particularly for island nations like Japan, it's important that we stay connected despite geographic and topographical hurdles.

USE TECHNOLOGY WISELY

I am a digital evangelist. Over the last 20 years, I have been convinced that technology is as much a source of opportunity and potential as it is of threat. As business leaders, we have a pivotal responsibility to ensure it is used and leveraged to help rather than hinder and doesn't exacerbate any of the problems already blighting the world. On this subject, too, I am a firm believer that Bushido can be a moral compass – a North Star – and specifically the virtue of self-control.

Technology is exciting. Innovation can be captivating. And when humans are excited, we quickly lose focus and get carried away. We really are quite simple creatures. So, as the CEO of Sompo, I try to lead by example in this respect. Specifically – and this relates directly back to what we have already discussed – I place a great emphasis on collaborating with some of the finest minds in the field, to ensure that we are navigating emerging technologies in the smartest possible way. It involves humility – knowing what we do not know – and it involves pragmatism. We must always consider how technology can enhance the quality of human life rather than inhibit or challenge it.

In 2019, we decided at Sompo to form a Japanese joint venture with the data analytics company Palantir Technologies Japan, initially to focus on creating new healthcare solutions for our clients.

Palantir is a fascinating business. It was founded in 2003 by a group of entrepreneurs and venture capitalists, including Peter Thiel and Alex Carp, who were convinced the technology products on the market at that time were either too rigid to handle novel problems or too complex to deploy.[67] The existing automated technologies, the company explains on its website, "failed against adaptive adversaries" and relied on "all-or-nothing access controls that forced organizations to make unacceptable trade-offs between collaborating and securing sensitive data from misuse."[68]

I admire Peter, Alex and their team for demonstrating at least some of the principles of Bushido as they launched their venture. Most obviously, they were courageous and bold: they spotted a problem facing the world, and they were determined to fix it.

Sompo's collaboration with Palantir is a 50-50 joint venture that serves commercial clients as well as the Japanese government. We feel privileged to be in a partnership with such a dynamic, cutting-edge player, but what we value most about Palantir as a business is its commitment to ensuring technology will always be a force for good.

I urge all business leaders to be scrutinous and critical when evaluating the ways in which they use technology and the reasons they do so. Every business will have a different need for technology. Good leadership is about recognizing that need and meeting it in an efficient and responsible way that considers every implication for every stakeholder.

THE DATA WE GATHER
INSPIRES INNOVATIVE
SERVICES TO BENEFIT
CUSTOMERS WHEN
ACCIDENTS AND ILLNESS
OCCUR, BUT ALSO TO
ENHANCE WELLBEING
AND HAPPINESS.
WE TRANSFORM REAL
DATA INTO A TRULY
VALUABLE RESOURCE.

UNDERSTAND DATA AS A PRECIOUS COMMODITY

Data is, of course, closely related to technology, but it nonetheless merits a few separate and specific considerations of its own. Off the back of our joint venture with Palantir, we announced in 2020 that we would jointly be launching what we have coined the *Real Data Platform for Security, Health and Wellbeing*.

As well as insurance businesses, our group is engaged in the nursing care and healthcare business. Through these businesses, we garner huge volumes of real data on accidents, disasters and other matters. We can use this data not only to pay benefits when accidents and illness occur but also to provide solutions that prevent accidents and illness. In this way, we aim to transform our real data into a truly valuable resource.

Across Japan and far beyond, industries as diverse as healthcare, automotive and manufacturing have generated a vast amount of data over the past few decades, and the volume of that data continues to expand exponentially every day. We've been determined to ensure that, as the data available to us grows, our scope and ability to handle it and use it intelligently keeps pace, too.

Through investing in innovative startups and by developing our own ways of handling the waves of information that we can collect, we've already been able to achieve remarkable feats. One project supported by the Real Data Platform, for example, is educating us about the risks of natural disasters occurring and what infrastructural measures can be put in place now to save lives in future. We've also been able to analyse and synthesize historical data on weather patterns to determine what agricultural yields will look like in years to come.

COVID-19 has, of course, shone a light on other ways in which real data can and should be used in future. It should help us determine how pandemics spread and how we can protect ourselves from infections in future. And it should be able to help us avert shutdowns of global supply chains, like the ones we experienced in 2020.

Of course here, too, we're only at the very beginning. Our understanding and power to handle data is nascent. But the potential is limitless, and we're convinced that data already is and will continue to be a commodity as valuable as gold or crude oil in the years and decades ahead.

DON'T OVERLOOK WHAT'S CLOSE TO HOME

At the beginning of this book, I shared my thoughts on the Great Acceleration and how the detrimental impacts that it has had on our society are often overlooked and neglected. One other habit that we as a society have developed as a result of the Great Acceleration is to be quickly charmed by something happening away from us. Though I'm not a fan of clichés, the old adage of the grass always being greener on the other side springs to mind.

Our attention spans have shortened since the advent of social media, and we're quick to turn our attention to the most spectacular headline, most bold claim or most promising prospect. I can't help but think of the rise in the popularity of cryptocurrency. It started as the domain of data nerds and computer geeks, but as soon as the first big headlines about Bitcoin millionaires emerged, it felt like people in every industry across every country of the world were trying to get involved, throwing their money at something that few of them really understood.

As the world has sped up, we've become impulsive and much less discerning than we used to be, and that has caused us to lose perspective. In some cases, we've even forgotten what we really care about: where real value lies.

I am guilty of committing this mistake, too. Especially early in my career, I was dazzled by the West. I was hypnotized by what was happening in places like Silicon Valley, New York and the capital cities of Europe. I had this misinformed idea in my head that, to be a successful businessperson, I would have to emulate the culture of the West. I wanted to find the Western elixir, bring it back to Japan and thrive.

But as I traveled the world, gathered experiences and matured considerably, I understood how foolish that myopic focus was. I had been so close to the Eastern – and particularly the Japanese – way of living and doing business that I had come to take it for granted.

This relates back to authenticity, the fifth value of Bushido. We can't spend our lives and careers trying to distance ourselves from a culture that we have become accustomed to and trying to replace it with something that we don't truly know or understand.

I urge you to check yourself constantly. What are the values that have shaped you and that have helped you to develop into the leader you are today? Where did those values come from? How can you draw on your experiences to improve or mold those values while not dismantling them completely? And where might you seek inspiration to do so? These are questions we should regularly ask ourselves.

CELEBRATE YOUR OWN REBEL

On the very first page of this book, I gave you a rare glimpse into my childhood. If you look at me today, you might be amused to think of me as the troublesome schoolboy or the pigheaded college student. But I frequently dwell on those images with a sense of both amusement and pride. That's because I know that who I was then determined who I later became and who I am today.

While I truly believe that there are many great things about the Japanese way of living, and the virtues of Bushido should form the bedrock of business culture not just in this country, I think we would all benefit, and particularly in this country, of fostering a slightly rebellious streak a little more.

Of course, I'm not endorsing rebellion for the sake of rebellion. There's never an excuse for thoughtless disobedience or lawlessness, but we should never be afraid to question why we are doing something the way we are doing it and to challenge that if we can't find an answer.

The parameters of the working world have, in many industries, gone unquestioned for decades, even centuries, but to live our best lives, be the best leaders and provide as much value as possible to all our stakeholders, we must be comfortable scrutinizing these and challenging them where appropriate.

Once again, authenticity is paramount. You need to find your own version of rebellion, and refine and practice that in a way that makes sense for you and your organization. In Japan, we've historically been excellent at taking a model and copying it perfectly – be that in retail or technology – but that's not possible here. There's no blueprint or manual. Having a relentlessly critical mind and being able to reflect on your own actions and decisions, though, is a skill that can be learned and perfected with hard work and persistence. There's a rebel inside all of us. The art lies in knowing how and when to let it out.

I am truly grateful for having the opportunity to tell my story, the story of Sompo, and for having the chance to interpret the code of Bushido for the modern world, based on my own experiences. As leaders, we are challenged from every angle. But at Sompo we are laser-focused on providing social value that contributes to building a sustainable society.

In the future, businesses should focus on long-term corporate actions that create social value and enhance the sustainability of human society. Some signs of progress are emerging, such as attempts to create a framework for sustainability reporting, but we still have a lot of work to do. The spirit of Bushido and the values that Bushido encompasses will enhance such actions for the common good.

The world continues to develop and innovate at a rapid clip and our ability to make decisions quickly has never been more important. But as we do so, it's also never been more important to pause and consider our values, our purposes and why we really do what we do every single day.

We need to keep focused on what we hope to pass on to those who follow in our footsteps. What will our legacy be? What problems will our children and their children inherit from us? What solutions can we develop and what habits can we adopt that will ensure a safe and prosperous future for them?

The pandemic forced us to slow down but let us maintain the courage to decelerate. We must acknowledge and understand that reducing our pace and thinking again yields immeasurable riches. The world will thank us.

THE WAY WE LIVE AND WHAT WE DO MUST ALIGN WITH WHAT IS RESPONSIBLE, ETHICAL AND SUSTAINABLE.

PART 4:
SUMMARY

To truly succeed, be that as an individual or a corporation, we must learn to appreciate cooperation as well as competition. The power of collaboration was demonstrated explicitly during the COVID-19 pandemic. We'd be foolish not to take those lessons to heart.

We must also learn to master the balancing act between ambition and realism. To promote the concept of the entrepreneur but not get lost in the fiction attached to the label, and appreciate the hard work, dedication and great challenges faced in running a business.

We must understand and accept the unusual and, sometimes, counterintuitive outputs of technology.

Finally, we must be open-minded, constantly curious and unafraid of experimentation. The value of an inner rebel should never, ever be underestimated.

PART 5

THE SOMPO MANIFESTO FOR A SUSTAINABLE FUTURE

Having discussed the issues around business transformation and the Bushido philosophy, I am very conscious that one of the great challenges of running a business is taking concepts and ideas and turning them into reality.

Accordingly, and as a final contribution to this book, I would like to share with you the Sompo Manifesto, which guides us on a daily basis.

- Embrace the virtues and benefits of Security, Health and Wellbeing and the Sompo concept of a 'Theme Park' of diverse products for customers.

- Adapt and follow the principle of Bushido to provide social value that contributes to building a sustainable future (Sustainable Development Goals) and show commitment to society.

- Adopt the business principle of Sampo – Yoshi – success through responsibility and achieving three-way satisfaction for the seller, buyer and broader society.

- Re-engineer the business to fully embrace and address climate change. Reject greenwashing or tokenism – positive action!

- Value collaboration over competition. Celebrate value in all that we do.

- Use technology wisely. Understand data as a precious commodity. Preserve customer confidentiality at all times.

- Do not overlook what is close to home. Think big!

- Celebrate your own rebel. Lead by example.

JOIN
US?

ACKNOWLEDGMENTS

I would like to thank all those who have supported me in writing this book.

The idea originated out of discussions with my colleague, Nigel Frudd, who felt strongly that the solution to re-engineering businesses worldwide, post-COVID-19, may be found closer to home – in the Japanese concept of Bushido, on which this book is based.

I would also like to acknowledge the great support and contributions I have received from my board, the members of which wanted the Sompo philosophy to be explained to the world. And I would also like to thank our customers, partners and stakeholders for their continued support.

My final thanks go to the hardworking colleagues within Sompo worldwide, who have really outperformed during the pandemic, thus showing the true working principles of Bushido. Without them, nothing would be possible.

ENDNOTES

1. Keynes, John Maynard. *The General Theory of Employment, Interest, and Money*. New York: Macmillan. 1936. https://www.palgrave.com/gp/book/9783319703435. Accessed 12 January 2021.

2. Nitobe, Inazo. Bushido: The Soul Of Japan. Kodansha America. 2012.

3. Strauss, William and Howe, Neil. *Generations: The History of America's Future, 1584 to 2069*. New York: HarperCollins. 1991. https://www.harpercollins.com/products/generations-neil-howewilliam-strauss. Accessed 22 December 2020.

4. Tversky, Amos and Kahneman, Daniel. *Thinking, Fast and Slow*. New York: Macmillan. 1994. https://us.macmillan.com/books/9780374533557. Accessed 22 December 2020.

5. Clinton, Hillary. "Moving Beyond Quarterly Capitalism". Medium. 2015. https://medium.com/hillary-for-america/moving-beyond-quarterly-capitalism-7abec53733f6. Accessed 22 December 2020.

6. Johnson, Joseph. "Worldwide digital population as of January 2021". Statista. 24 November 2020. https://www.statista.com/statistics/617136/digital-population-worldwide/. Accessed 10 January 2021.

7. Ibid.

8. Konok, Veronika., Gigler, Dóra., Bereczky, Boróka Mária and Miklosi, Adam. "Humans' attachment to their mobile phones and its relationship with interpersonal attachment style". Computers in Human Behavior.

August 2016. https://www.researchgate.net/publication/299472808_
Humans'_attachment_to_their_mobile_phones_and_its_relationship_
with_interpersonal_attachment_style. Accessed 9 January 2021.

9. Wigglesworth, Robin. "US stocks' record bull run brought to abrupt
end by coronavirus". Financial Times. 12 March 2020. https://www.
ft.com/content/6b987f46-644f-11ea-b3f3-fe4680ea68b5. Accessed
10 January 2021.

10. Dittmann, M. "Standing tall pays off, study finds". Monitor on
Psychology. July 2004. https://www.apa.org/monitor/julaug04/
standing. Accessed 31 March 2021.

11. Whitting, Kate. "5 shocking facts about inequality, according to
Oxfam's latest report". World Economic Forum. 20 January 2020.
https://www.weforum.org/agenda/2020/01/5-shocking-facts-
about-inequality-according-to-oxfam-s-latest-report/. Accessed
9 January 2021.

12. Vandivier, David. "What is The Great Gatsby Curve?". Whitehouse.
gov. 11 June 2013. https://obamawhitehouse.archives.gov/
blog/2013/06/11/what-great-gatsby-curve. Accessed 9 January 2021.

13. Schaeffer, Katherine. "6 facts about economic inequality in the U.S.".
Pew Research Centre. 7 February 2020. https://www.pewresearch.org/
fact-tank/2020/02/07/6-facts-about-economic-inequality-in-the-u-s/.
Accessed 10 January 2021.

14. Cox, Josie. "New Research Shows Covid-19's Impact On Gender
Inequality And Mothers' Mental Health". Forbes. 30 July 2020.
https://www.forbes.com/sites/josiecox/2020/07/30/covid-19-gender-
equality-mental-health-working-mothers-flexible-working/. Accessed
31 March 2021.

15. "COVID-19 Racial and Ethnic Disparities". Centre for Disease
Control and Prevention. 10 December 2020. https://www.cdc.gov/
coronavirus/2019-ncov/community/health-equity/racial-ethnic-
disparities/index.html. Accessed 31 March 2021.

16. Blawatt, Ken R. *Marconomics: Defining Economics through Social Science
and Consumer Behavior*. Bingley: Emerald Group Publishing Limited. 2016.
https://www.emerald.com/insight/content/doi/10.1108/978-1-78635-
566-920161009/full/pdf?title=prelims. Accessed 10 January 2021.

17. McNeill, Kirsty and Jacobs, Corry. "Half of the world's population lack access to essential health services – are we doing enough?". World Economic Forum. 20 September 2019. https://www.weforum.org/agenda/2019/09/half-of-the-world-s-population-lack-access-to-essential-health-services-are-we-doing-enough/. Accessed 11 January 2021.

18. Sakurada, Kengo. "Redesign Capitalism to Incorporate Social Value". Time Magazine. 22 October 2020, https://time.com/collection/great-reset/5901668/content-from-sompo-social-value/. Accessed 10 January 2021.

19. "Climate Change: How do we know?". NASA: Global Climate Change. 9 January 2021. https://climate.nasa.gov/evidence/. Accessed 9 January 2021.

20. Workman, James. "'Our house is on fire.' 16 year-old Greta Thunberg wants action". World Economic Forum. 25 January 2019. https://www.weforum.org/agenda/2019/01/our-house-is-on-fire-16-year-old-greta-thunberg-speaks-truth-to-power/. Accessed 9 January 2021.

21. Watson, Bruce. "The troubling evolution of corporate greenwashing". The Guardian. 20 August 2016. https://www.theguardian.com/sustainable-business/2016/aug/20/greenwashing-environmentalism-lies-companies. Accessed 31 March 2021.

22. Gore, Al and Guggenheim, Davis. *An Inconvenient Truth*. Lawrence Bender Productions. 24 May 2006. https://www.imdb.com/title/tt0497116/. Accessed 31 March 2021.

23. Solly, Meilan. "Carbon Dioxide Levels Reach Highest Point in Human History". Smithsonian Magazine. 15 May 2019. https://www.smithsonianmag.com/smart-news/carbon-dioxide-levels-reach-highest-point-human-history-180972181/. Accessed 31 March 2021.

24. Khokhar, Tariq and Tabary, Mahyar Eshragh. "Five forest figures for the International Day of Forests". World Bank Blogs. 21 March 2016. https://blogs.worldbank.org/opendata/five-forest-figures-international-day-forests. Accessed 31 March 2021.

25. La Duke, Phil. "If 80 Percent of Success Is Showing Up Then 20 Percent Is Following Up". Entrepreneur Europe. 8 November 2016. https://www.entrepreneur.com/article/282745. Accessed 31 March 2021.

26. Gallagher, Chris. "In Japan, 'Rocky' and 'Premium Friday' join fight against overtime". Reuters. 24 February 2017. https://www.reuters.com/article/us-japan-overwork-reforms/in-japan-rocky-and-premium-friday-join-fight-against-overtime-idUSKBN1630OC. Accessed 31 March 2021.

27. "How Robots Change the World: What Automation Really Means for Jobs and Productivity". Oxford Economics. June 2019. https://cdn2.hubspot.net/hubfs/2240363/Report%20-%20How%20Robots%20Change%20the%20World.pdf. Accessed 9 January 2021.

28. Flemming, Sean. "This is the world's biggest mental health problem – and you might not have heard of it". World Economic Forum. 14 January 2019, https://www.weforum.org/agenda/2019/01/this-is-the-worlds-biggest-mental-health-problem/. Accessed 10 January 2021.

29. Kelland, Kate. "Mental health crisis could cost the world $16 trillion by 2030". Reuters. 9 October 2018. https://www.reuters.com/article/us-health-mental-global/mental-health-crisis-could-cost-the-world-16-trillion-by-2030-idUSKCN1MJ2QN. Accessed 10 January 2021.

30. "Life expectancy at birth, total (years)". The World Bank. https://data.worldbank.org/indicator/SP.DYN.LE00.IN. Accessed 11 January 2021.

31. "The Human Genome Project". National Human Genome Research Institute. https://www.genome.gov/human-genome-project. Accessed 11 January 2021.

32. "The History of the Electric Car". The United States Department of Energy. 15 September 2014. https://www.energy.gov/articles/history-electric-car. Accessed 11 January 2021.

33. "20 years already? Alan Greenspan and the 'irrational exuberance' flop". MarketWatch. 6 December 2016. https://www.marketwatch.com/story/20-years-already-alan-greenspan-and-the-irrational-exuberance-flop-2016-12-05. Accessed 31 March 2021.

34. Stiglitz, Joseph. *People, Power, and Profits: Progressive Capitalism for an Age of Discontent*. New York: W. W. Norton & Company. 2019. https://wwnorton.com/books/People-Power-and-Profits/. Accessed 31 March 2021.

35. Kennedy, Robert F. "Remarks at the University of Kansas, March 18, 1968". John F Kennedy Library. https://www.jfklibrary.org/learn/about-jfk/the-kennedy-family/robert-f-kennedy/robert-f-kennedy-speeches/remarks-at-the-university-of-kansas-march-18-1968. Accessed 31 March 2021.

36. Khan, Natasha. "New Virus Discovered by Chinese Scientists Investigating Pneumonia Outbreak". The Wall Street Journal. 8 January 2020. https://www.wsj.com/articles/new-virus-discovered-by-chinese-scientists-investigating-pneumonia-outbreak-11578485668. Accessed 11 January 2021.

37. Ghebreyesus, Dr Tedros Adhanom. "WHO Director-General's opening remarks at the media at the media briefing on COVID-19 - 11 March 2020". World Health Organisation. 11 March 2020. https://www.who.int/director-general/speeches/detail/who-director-general-s-opening-remarks-at-the-media-briefing-on-covid-19-11-march-2020. Accessed 11 January 2021.

38. Cox, Josie. "New Research Shows Covid-19's Impact On Gender Inequality and Mothers' Mental Health". Forbes. 30 July 2020. https://www.forbes.com/sites/josiecox/2020/07/30/covid-19-gender-equality-mental-health-working-mothers-flexible-working/. Accessed 11 January 2021.

39. Sprechmann, Sofia. "COVID-19 is the biggest setback to gender equality in a decade". World Economic Forum. 1 July 2020. https://www.weforum.org/agenda/2020/07/gender-equality-women-employment-covid19/. Accessed 11 January 2021.

40. Madgavkar, Anu., White, Olivia., Krishnan., Mahajan, Deepa and Azcue, Xavier. "COVID-19 and gender equality: Countering the regressive effects". 15 July 2020. https://www.mckinsey.com/featured-insights/future-of-work/covid-19-and-gender-equality-countering-the-regressive-effects. Accessed 11 January 2021.

41. Triggs, Adam and Kharas, Homi. "The triple economic shock of COVID-19 and priorities for an emergency G-20 leaders meeting". Brookings. 17 March 2020. https://www.brookings.edu/blog/future-development/2020/03/17/the-triple-economic-shock-of-covid-19-and-priorities-for-an-emergency-g-20-leaders-meeting/. Accessed 11 January 2021.

42. Newcomb, Alyssa. "Super Strength: Daughter Rescues Dad Pinned Under Car". ABC News. 1 August 2012. https://abcnews.go.com/US/superhero-woman-lifts-car-off-dad/story?id=16907591. Accessed 11 January 2021.

43. "Man lifts car off pinned cyclist". Tucson.com. 28 July 2006. https://tucson.com/news/local/crime/man-lifts-car-off-pinned-cyclist/article_e7f04bbd-309b-5c7e-808d-1907d91517ac.html. Accessed 11 January 2021.

44. Abboud, Leila. "Inside the factory: how LVMH met France's call for hand sanitiser in 72 hours". Financial Times. 18 March 2020. https://www.ft.com/content/e9c2bae4-6909-11ea-800d-da70cff6e4d3. Accessed 31 March 2021.

45. "Ford Coronavirus Updates". Ford Media Center. https://media.ford.com/content/fordmedia/fna/us/en/media-kits/2020/ford-corona-virus-updates.html. Accessed 31 March 2021.

46. "Airbus plans to further adapt to COVID-19 environment". Airbus Newsroom. 30 June 2020. https://www.airbus.com/newsroom/press-releases/en/2020/06/airbus-plans-to-further-adapt-to-covid19-environment.html. Accessed 31 March 2021.

47. Giles, Sunnie. "How VUCA Is Reshaping The Business Environment, And What It Means for Innovation". Forbes. 9 May 2018. https://www.forbes.com/sites/sunniegiles/2018/05/09/how-vuca-is-reshaping-the-business-environment-and-what-it-means-for-innovation/. Accessed 11 January 2021.

48. Caryl-Sue. "Mar 11, 2011 CE: Tohoku Earthquake and Tsunami". National Geographic. 6 April 2020. https://www.nationalgeographic.org/thisday/mar11/tohoku-earthquake-and-tsunami/. Accessed 31 March 2021.

49. "Japan quake: Worst crisis since WWII, says PM". BBC News. 14 March 2011. https://www.bbc.com/news/world-asia-pacific-12726297. Accessed 31 March 2021.

50. "Origin and meaning of honor". Online Etymology Dictionary. https://www.etymonline.com/word/honor. Accessed 31 March 2021.

51. "Coronavirus Disease (COVID-19) Situation Reports." World Health Organization. 2020–21. https://www.who.int/emergencies/diseases/novel-coronavirus-2019/situation-reports. Accessed 13 January 2021.

52. Schumpeter, Joseph. *Capitalism, Socialism and Democracy*. New York: Harper & Brothers. 1942.

53. Kahneman, Daniel. *Thinking, Fast and Slow*. New York: Farrar, Straus and Giroux. 2011.

54. Friedman, Milton. "A Friedman doctrine – The Social Responsibility Of Business Is To Increase Its Profits". The New York Times. 13 September 1970. https://www.nytimes.com/1970/09/13/archives/a-friedman-doctrine-the-social-responsibility-of-business-is-to.html. Accessed 15 January 2021.

55. "Business Roundtable Redefines the Purpose of a Corporation to Promote 'An Economy That Serves All Americans'". Business Roundtable. 19 August 2019. https://www.businessroundtable.org/business-roundtable-redefines-the-purpose-of-a-corporation-to-promote-an-economy-that-serves-all-americans. Accessed 15 January 2021.

56. Fink, Larry. "Larry Fink's Letter to CEOs". BlackRock, Inc. January 2021. https://www.blackrock.com/corporate/investor-relations/larry-fink-ceo-letter. Accessed 15 January 2021.

57. Schwab, Klaus. "The Fourth Industrial Revolution: what it means and how to respond". World Economic Forum. 14 January 2016. https://www.weforum.org/agenda/2016/01/the-fourth-industrial-revolution-what-it-means-and-how-to-respond/. Accessed 15 January 2021.

58. Jaschik, Scott. "Humanities Majors Drop". Inside Higher Education. 5 June 2017. https://www.insidehighered.com/news/2017/06/05/analysis-finds-significant-drop-humanities-majors-gains-liberal-arts-degrees. Accessed 31 March 2021.

59. Sears, Alan and Clark, Penney. "Stop telling students to study STEM instead of humanities for the post-coronavirus world". The Conversation. 28 September 2020. https://theconversation.com/stop-telling-students-to-study-stem-instead-of-humanities-for-the-post-coronavirus-world-145813. Accessed 31 March 2021.

60. Carnegie, Dale. *How to win friends and influence people*. Rev. ed. New York: Simon and Schuster. 1981.

61. Garner, Dwight. "Classic Advice: Please, Leave Well Enough Alone". The New York Times. 5 October 2011. https://www.nytimes.com/2011/10/05/books/books-of-the-times-classic-advice-please-leave-well-enough-alone.html. Accessed 31 March 2021.

62. "About us". Panasonic.com". https://www.panasonic.com/global/corporate/history/konosuke-matsushita/story2-06.html. Accessed 31 March 2021.

63. Ibid.

64. Schwab, Klaus. *COVID-19: The Great Reset*. Geneva: Agentur Schweiz. 2020.

65. Thunberg, Greta. *No One Is Too Small to Make a Difference*. New York: Penguin Books. 2019.

66. Mazzucato, Mariana. *Mission Economy: A Moonshot Guide to Changing Capitalism*. New York: Penguin Books Limited. 2021.

67. "About". Plantir.com. https://www.palantir.com/about/. Accessed 31 March 2021.

68. Ibid.